The Hungry Brain

Laura Pawlak, Ph.D.

To my parents
for life, learning, and love.

To my animal companions.
Life's journey together – priceless.

Emily	Smee	Licorice
Jonathan	Hook	Belle
Phoenix	Napoleon	Starr
Heather	Bobbi	Radish
Jennifer	Noah	Sweet Pea
Salty	Angel	Oreo
Phoebe	Shallot	Blackberri
Samson	Cinnamon	Carrot

and future companions

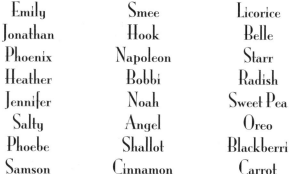

Apple

THE BRAIN

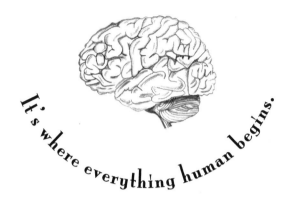

It's where everything human begins.

Editor: Richard S. Colman, Ph.D.

Copy Editor: Elizabeth Ohm

Cover Design: Biomed General

Illustrations & Layout Design: Erika Paras

Photos: By the Author

CONTENTS

Introduction
The Five *Hungers* of the Brain 9

Chapter One
PLEASURE:
Tempting Foods 15

Chapter Two
CALORIES:
Obesity and the Altered Brain 51

Chapter Three
PROTECTION:
Fat and the Brain 81

Chapter Four
MYSTERIOUS LINKS:
Nutrients and Neurons 113

Chapter Five
LONGEVITY:
**Nutrition and
the Prevention of Alzheimer's** 149

Resources 217

Glossary 219

Index 223

Critter Diary

As science opens the door to understanding what's inside your cranium, it's time to reminisce about the not-so-long-ago days of ignorance regarding the brain. This scenario is about my first dog, Jennifer, a sheep dog with an incredibly gentle spirit. Round and cuddly, she was my big, live teddy bear.

Jennifer abhorred exercise---after that frenzied puppy stage, of course. Living in a huge house with roommates, I was constantly chiding my co-inhabitants about giving her extra treats and table scraps. Luckily, the outdoor life in California kept her reasonably fit until I moved to the city for serious employment. Then Jennifer's roly-poly genes took over and her weight problem became a serious issue. Her preference to just sit in the car all day while I worked simply added momentum to her expanding fat cells.

As she grew old, I noticed she had a hard time finding our house, but I credited it to the huge amount of hair over her eyes and got a barrette to fix the problem. She was no better. Looking back, I realize Jennifer had signs of cognitive decline, or possibly worse.

Jennifer passed away thirty years ago. Scientists had not unraveled the essential position of nutrition in the prevention of Alzheimer's disease. Neuroscience has arrived and there are answers---for every brain.

Introduction
The Five *Hungers* of the Brain

Prevention is better than cure---especially for your brain.

The word *hunger* conveys a variety of meanings. You may imagine intense pangs of hunger for nourishment, recall the times your heart hungered for love, or smile about your childhood "Mom, please" hungers of the past.

Perhaps you have not described your brain as hungry, but it is. In fact, the brain has five hungers---pleasure, calories, protection, efficiency, and longevity---purposefully united. They optimize your brain's potential for survival.

Why aspire to optimize that four-pound mass within your cranium? There are no brain transplants. It's time to get serious about what's at the end of your fork.

Pleasure
It is the perk that leads to
curiosity, learning, and smarter survival---maybe.

Just as the moon affects ocean tides, feeling good is a powerful force that inspires learning. When good feelings are equated with food, you learn more is better. Surrounded by foods that ignite pleasure, the mind can easily capitulate. The will to reject tempting foods lies within your brain, not on the dinner table. Chapter One offers practical guidelines that empower your prefrontal cortex and improve your resistance to tempting foods that age your brain.

Calories

Absent the cycle of famine,
the brain is stuck in the "store more" mode,
with an endless supply of fat cells to do the job.

The dysfunction of excess adipose tissue---chronically enlarged fat cells---presents a unique health crisis. Chapter Two explains the dilemma of chronic overnutrition and the resultant decay of an organ that, ironically, doesn't store fat or use fat as fuel---your brain.

Will the shocking statistics linking obesity to Alzheimer's disease spur you to lose weight and keep it off? Participate in the Homework at the end of each chapter. You will lose weight.

Protection

The right fats combat the brain's sensitivity to chemical decay.

Negative moods are predictors of cognitive decline. Chapter Three has news about a mix of fluid fats that act as neuroprotectants and boosters for a better mood. Follow the various fats into your hungry brain and observe their actions---for better or worse.

Mysterious Links

A whole food creates greater efficiency
among neurons than its isolated nutrients. How mysterious!

The brain utilizes more energy than any other tissue. It is hungry for the oxygen you breathe and the nutrients you consume. Supplied with healthful nutrition, your neurons hum with efficiency.

Chapter Four describes the mysterious relationship of food nutrients to your brain's processing speed and explains how the various antioxidants, obtained from food, are linked to a youthful brain.

Longevity

You can live without intelligence, but what's the point?

At birth, every facet of brain activity reflects the hunger to learn and thus to survive. Life without memory processing, learning, and intellect is a fearful thought. Beyond obtaining the nutrients essential for hardworking neurons, the brain desperately needs your personal hunger to act against Alzheimer's disease.

Chapter Five begins with a tour of memory-making and the nutritional buffers against cognitive decline. The chapter presents the science supporting the statement: *Nutrition makes a difference in the longevity of your brain, beginning with your first spoonful of food*. Each brain-smart nutrient discussed in the text is translated into smart food choices and a grocery list---for the sake of your brain.

Conclusion

For a superbly efficient brain over the decades, refine your cerebral performance: Analyze the quality of the fuel you provide, the fats you devour, and the nutrients you ingest. You can successfully maneuver the brain's hunger for pleasure in a world of bewitching excess. *The Hungry Brain* is your "operator's guide" for the journey.

Reader's Notes

"MORE"

Beyond the scientific findings explored in the text, these inserts explain some fascinating facts and functions of your brain at a deeper, biochemical level.

"Critter Diary"

I have adopted the many animals you will meet in the text. Their stories add another dimension to your reading---flavor to the facts about your brain.

"What's the Point?"
A short diversion from the discussion at hand, What's The Point? paragraphs interrupt the text to expand your mind with news bites and questions to ponder.

"Homework"

Put the information into practice right away with meaningful work that brings home the qualities of a dynamic brain.

Abbreviations throughout the Text

AA	arachidonic acid
ALA	alpha linolenic acid
ApoE	apolipoprotein E
ATP	adenosine triphosphate
BDNF	brain-derived neurotrophic factor
DHA	docosahexaenoic acid
DPA	docosapentaenoic acid
EPA	eicosapentaenoic acid
GABA	gamma-aminobutyric acid
GLA	gamma linolenic acid
IU	international units
LA	linoleic acid
mcg	microgram
mg	milligram
ml	milliliter
MRI	magnetic resonance imaging
ng	nanogram
SAM-e	s-adenosylmethionine
UVA	ultraviolet A rays
UVB	ultraviolet B rays

Resources

Following Chapter Five, current popular publications, referenced throughout the text, provide further reading about the brain.

THE BRAIN

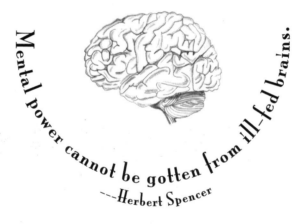

Mental power cannot be gotten from ill-fed brains.
---Herbert Spencer

Chapter One
Pleasure: Tempting Foods

Hardwired for Pleasure 16

Seeking Food 17
   Instinctual eating habits 17
   Beyond hunger pangs 18
   The seeking circuitry 20

Taste and Temptation 22
   The pleasure chemical 23
   Taste anomalies 24
   Your insula interprets tempting 28

Why I Want to Eat What I Eat 31

When Food Cravings Win 35
   Cognitive muscle training I 35
   Cognitive muscle training II 37

Tempting Foods: Are You Hooked? 40

Conclusion 42

Brain Homework: Nutrition for a Hungry Brain
   Take Charge: A Ten-Step Program 43

Key References 46

Everything in moderation.

---Aristotle

Hardwired for Pleasure

"They didn't fix my brain!" a profound statement from a woman saddened by a lifetime of obesity that even bariatric surgery could not fix. Following surgery, she continued to consume comforting foods---milk shakes and small bites of chocolate. Her stomach stretched, and with it, her body fat. What happened? It's about your brain's focus on survival, the perfect focus if you live in the Stone Age.

The human prefrontal cortex generates the power to dilute, rewire, or modify the dictates of an ancient emotional circuitry related to pleasure. Thought cannot, however, eliminate the urge to feel good. Positive feelings drive the desires of the human heart, whether you want alcohol, a chocolate cupcake, or hugs from a friend. Tempting foods are crafted to become your top choices as affordable, available, and acceptable pleasures.

This is not your ancestors' food, but you still have your ancestors' brain. And so, the battle begins---food cravings, food addictions, bingeing, or just plain overeating. The vast network that regulates energy intake with energy expenditure is designed to keep you within a potato chip of balance. Seeking food today as opposed to the yesterdays means using an outdated program for energy balance. It malfunctions when you eat junk food or endless amounts of sugar, fat, and salt in processed foods, even if they are organic.

Isn't it time to take charge of the foods you crave and reverse fat cells back to a reasonable size? This chapter demonstrates how tempting foods change your brain and presents ten steps that put you in charge. Even if you have always been lean, taking charge of tempting foods is still a priority---for a hungry brain.

Seeking Food

DOPAMINE MOLECULE

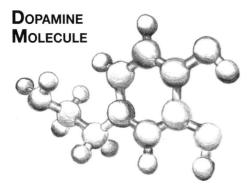

Persons with affluent lifestyles may never have experienced excruciating hunger, but everyone has cravings for l-o-v-e-d foods, unrelated to hunger. It's the dopamine spike from swallowing fat/sugar or fat/salt that captivates your mind---focus, search, reward.

Instinctual eating habits

The brain's survival instincts of the past are simply a nuisance today. Until recently, our ancestors could not count on the success of next year's harvest. Individuals lived the philosophy, *a bird in the hand is worth two in the bush*. This ancient instinct surfaces today with a similar slogan, *eat now, diet later*. The closer the tempting food, the harder it is to resist. Do you bring tempting foods into your home on a regular basis?

Physical work was a major part of the energy equation. You hunted and gathered, or planted and harvested. The entire regulatory machinery that triggers the brain's search for food is designed for active humans, imprinted with that lifestyle for thousands of years. Enter the couch potato, with sedentary behaviors unlike any time in history. No doubt, energy regulation will falter without real work. What's your real work?

Humans are opportunists. If given unplanned access to rich and appealing food, they tend to gorge. It's called the *dessert effect*. Long ago, when famine might be around the corner, or food was difficult to find, it was the smart thing to do. If the dessert effect hooks you, practice *cognitive muscle training*, on page 35.

Humans actively seek culinary variety, such as a buffet. You try everything, temporarily overriding regulatory signals. It seems impossible to curb yourself. Why? No single food contains all the nutrients required for life. Choosing a variety of foods is about survival. Your ancient genes haven't adapted to the all-you-can-eat buffet. Do your meals at home resemble a buffet, that is, too many choices?

Tempting foods, high in fat/sugar or fat/salt, are *unnatural* foods. You become desensitized to the cues of energy balance when the taste of the food is overwhelming. Do you make tempting foods at home, such as chocolate chip cookies or a fatty meat loaf? Make them with more healthful ingredients. The tempting foods are now less familiar and less emotionally comforting. You'll notice your instinct to eat them begins to wither away.

> **Take Charge!**
> *Get smart about your survival genes related to food ---or get drawn into the world of tempting foods.*

Beyond hunger pangs

Hunger instigates bodily arousal. The mind dismisses the sensations that cue a need for food. The growing discomfort triggers an irresistable desire for a tempting food. The search begins.

Why is the urge to eat so frequent and insistent when the body stores plenty of calories as fat? The life-sustaining fuel for the brain is carbohydrates. You can't convert fats to carbohydrates. You can sever fat into small molecules called *ketone bodies* when carbohydrates are scarce, but the brain is less efficient when the fuel source is ketones.

Critter Diary

I can remember experiencing extreme hunger and thirst during a safari in Tanzania, East Africa. The safari truck got separated from the supply van, with no means of communication between the two vehicles. Six tourists on safari, all well nourished, set up camp. As the wait for supplies proceeded from day one to day two, the group leader asked everyone to deposit their food and water in community containers. The small amount of water was rationed and the food distributed by handfuls. I observed tour companions stealthily hoarding food. Two men illegally killed a zebra and cooked it over an open fire. Survival dominated their thoughts and behaviors.

By the end of day three, the group voted to load up the truck and seek food. After a long, hot day in the desert sun, hunger and thirst saturated my whole being. Binoculars in hand, I scanned the endless desert hoping to see a palm tree, another truck, animals, any life. Finally, a speck of green appeared on the horizon. The anticipation of food and water gave second wind to this very exhausted mind and body.

After a few bites of food and a big glass of water, my nervous energy evaporated. I sank into the sand, deep in thought. I had never realized how great it feels to be nourished and hydrated.

Tempting food is comforting food. According to Jaak Panksepp, author of *Affective Neuroscience*, seeking and consuming great-tasting food replaces negative emotions (fear, distress, anger) with good feelings. Even physical distress is diminished by comfort food. Kids learn this lesson at an early age.

Take Charge!
If you don't deal with your fears, distress, anger, or sadness, comfort food will.

What's the Point?
Little Lulu falls and scratches her knee. She runs to Mom. "It hurts," she cries. Mom bandages the wound, but what will erase the pain and make Lulu feel good again? A cookie! The anticipation of Mom's homemade cookies---dopamine. The fat and sugar in the cookie elicits endorphins.

Decades later, Lulu comes home from work with a heavy heart. Her lifelong companion has passed away. She opens the freezer, but nothing is appetizing until she sees the cookie dough. It's the perfect remedy for a heartache!

The seeking circuitry

Dopamine-producing neurons form a series of tracts in the brain that coordinate an emotional response---seeking. Considering the basic need for nourishment, the entire seeking system is organized to integrate rational, motor, emotional, and hormonal factors to assure the search for food is successful.

These tracts can be sensitized by the sound, sight, feel, aroma, or taste of a food. The mere memory of a tempting food can activate receptors on these dopamine-producing neurons and ignite a pursuit for the food reward. Anticipation of the pleasureful experience, focus on the goal, and action are then perpetuated by the hormone cortisol.

THE SEEKING SYSTEM

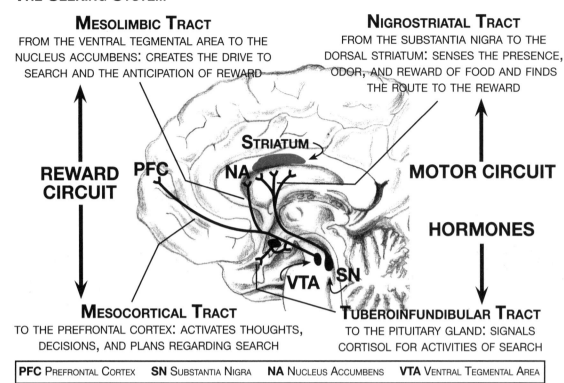

MESOLIMBIC TRACT
FROM THE VENTRAL TEGMENTAL AREA TO THE
NUCLEUS ACCUMBENS: CREATES THE DRIVE TO
SEARCH AND THE ANTICIPATION OF REWARD

NIGROSTRIATAL TRACT
FROM THE SUBSTANTIA NIGRA TO THE
DORSAL STRIATUM: SENSES THE PRESENCE,
ODOR, AND REWARD OF FOOD AND FINDS
THE ROUTE TO THE REWARD

REWARD CIRCUIT

PFC

STRIATUM

NA

MOTOR CIRCUIT

HORMONES

VTA **SN**

MESOCORTICAL TRACT
TO THE PREFRONTAL CORTEX: ACTIVATES THOUGHTS,
DECISIONS, AND PLANS REGARDING SEARCH

TUBEROINFUNDIBULAR TRACT
TO THE PITUITARY GLAND: SIGNALS
CORTISOL FOR ACTIVITIES OF SEARCH

PFC PREFRONTAL CORTEX	**SN** SUBSTANTIA NIGRA	**NA** NUCLEUS ACCUMBENS	**VTA** VENTRAL TEGMENTAL AREA

There are two tracts in the reward circuit: one tract leads to feelings (the *mesolimbic tract*), and the other to thoughts (the *mesocortical tract*). The *ventral tegmental area* is a group of dopamine-producing neurons, a nucleus, that initiates the entire reward circuit. As a search is sparked, one tract ends in the *nucleus accumbens*, releasing feel-good chemicals. The other tract terminates in the prefrontal cortex with a burst of positive thoughts.

The *substantia nigra* is another dopamine-producing nucleus that lies close to, and interacts with, the ventral tegmental area. This nucleus is the origin of a motor tract that refines movement for any search. The end point, the *striatum*, assesses the value of a reward.

For example, as you eat a food, the striatum generates an appraisal. When the actual pleasure is disappointing as compared to the anticipated reward, the motor pathway remains active. You are tempted to eat until your expectation is met. The number and activity of dopamine-producing neurons in the striatum---a factor of inheritance---affects this value assessment. Genetics thus plays a role in the amount of tempting food consumed.

Seeking is a finely tuned survival response. Brain structures outside the seeking system interact with the circuitry, improving the efficiency of a search. The amygdala retrieves pertinent emotional information about the search as well as any emotional memories related to past experiences. The hippocampus stores the map to the rewarding food and all cognitive information related to the experience.

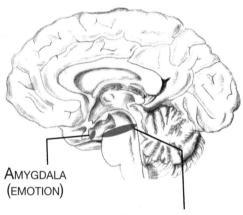

STRUCTURES AIDING THE SEEKING CIRCUITRY

AMYGDALA
(EMOTION)

HIPPOCAMPUS
(MEMORY OF INFORMATION)

Taste and Temptation

A twenty-four-hour fast creates genuine hunger. Yet, if the person is offered bland vs. tasty food following a fast, less of the bland food is consumed than the tasty choice. The amount of bland food consumed represents true energy balance. The amount of tasty food consumed varies with heredity, experiences, and the momentary sensory appeal---sparked by opioids, namely beta-endorphins.

Critter Diary

Apple is a very active cattle dog. She runs for hours each day and gets genuinely hungry. I feed her dry dog food. Because the food has no hedonic appeal, it can be available all the time. She eats small amounts when she is hungry and leaves the rest. If I add chicken broth to the food, she eats the entire amount at once and wants more---tasty food. Tasty equals overeating, especially when you are hungry.

The pleasure chemical

What feels better: anticipating an event or experiencing the event? If you conduct a survey, you may find the results are about even. In the context of food, some persons enjoy the expectation of a romantic dinner and the perfect ending---dessert. Others are simply annoyed if immediate gratification is not available. It's all about your brain chemicals.

Neuroscientists agree that experiencing pleasure while consuming a tempting food ultimately reflects the action of opioids in the brain. Imaging studies verify that activation of dopamine-producing neurons throughout the seeking circuitry precedes gratifying feelings. Brain maps thus support the role of dopamine as motivational and beta-endorphins as pleasureful chemicals.

Endorphin-mediated reward is a key ingredient in the desire for tempting food, the drive for sex, strong maternal behavior, and any social interaction involving touch. If the receptors for beta-endorphins are blocked, pleasure is nullified, supporting the endorphin-reward connection---with one caveat.

A large body of evidence indicates a reciprocal reward-related interaction between cannabinoids and opioids. Block receptors for cannabinoids and the rewarding feelings generated by opioids are inhibited.

What's the Point?
The mechanism underlying the relationship between opioids and cannabinoids is not clear. Still, knowing there is a positive association between the neurons generating these two substances opens the door to understanding issues beyond food---the subtle, addictive qualities of marijuana and its use for pain relief.

cannabinoids → opioids

pain relief
feel good/feel peaceful

Cannabinoids produced within the body and brain are called *endocannabinoids*. Human cells have specific receptors that recognize plant cannabinoid substances in marijuana and endogenous cannabinoids, such as *anandamide*. The endocannabinoid system is hyperactive in obese persons. These molecules awaken the appetite and enhance the conversion of glucose to stored fat.

The caloric value of tempting foods is simply part of a much greater issue. The endocannabinoids released as these loved foods are consumed provide a "feel-good" mood along with a chemical drive for more tempting foods. If you are living this scenario, willpower may vanish while weight gain waits just around the corner!

Taste anomalies

Food is a mixture of hundreds of chemicals. The food chemicals that produce taste activate specific receptors in the mouth. When a food chemical fits into a taste receptor, an impulse may travel along nerve fibers to the brain for interpretation, if there is enough activity in the receptor.

Thus, recognizing a particular taste varies with each individual, depending upon the number of receptors available for the food chemical, the concentration of the chemical in the mouth, and the influence of other senses, such as the aroma and texture of the food.

WHAT DO YOU TASTE?

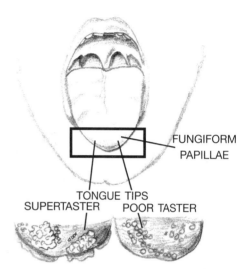

About twenty-five percent of any population has a greater-than-average number of taste buds; these people are called *supertasters*. An equal number have poor taste perception, regardless of age. Supertasters tend to be picky eaters. They are keenly aware of every subtle taste, texture, or aroma and generally eat less than poor tasters.

The brain perceives five tastes: sweet, sour, bitter, salty, and umami (the savory taste of meat). For decades scientists stated that fat was a carrier for different elements in food but had no independent signal in taste buds. Researchers now verify that fat causes electrical changes in the buds.

If you're not fooled by a fat-free version of your favorite fatty food, your taste buds are simply doing their job. Fat-free foods are unlikely to be as tempting as fatty foods because an important signal to the brain is missing---fat.

Why does a sweet taste make just about everyone smile? Sweetness innately produces brain opioids. Do artificial sweeteners have the same effect on the brain?

Both sucrose (a natural sweetener) and sucralose (an artificial sweetener) excite receptors in taste buds and signal the brain through the same primary taste pathways. Functional imaging of the brain reveals quality differences, however, between the real and fake sweeteners.

Guido Frank and coworkers found that the brain distinguishes the caloric from the non-caloric sweetener, although the conscious mind does not. Compared to sucralose, sugar elicits a greater positive response in two areas of the brain: the structure that generates bodily and emotional feelings, called the *insula*; and the structure determining the relative value of a perception, the *striatum*.

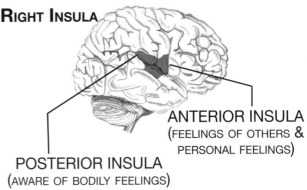

RIGHT INSULA

ANTERIOR INSULA
(FEELINGS OF OTHERS & PERSONAL FEELINGS)

POSTERIOR INSULA
(AWARE OF BODILY FEELINGS)

Data from studies of bulimia identify the release of opioids as a pleasure factor during the consumption of fatty foods, not just sweets. A craving for French fries or chips is as common as the passion for ice cream or candy. The thousands of calories consumed during a binge is an exaggerated response to the innate drive to live beyond the natural recurrence of famine. Genes related to survival of all species influence, but do not control, the consumption of food loaded with fat and/or sugar. If a person expresses few opioid receptors and/or opioid molecules, a hefty load of tempting food is required to achieve sufficient endorphin activity and merit a "wow" rating. The lifestyle factor---taking charge---is challenging, but possible, in a world designed to prepare your fat cells for famine and reward you for accomplishing the goal.

> **What's the Point?**
> *According to Sarah Leibowitz, neurobiologist at Rockefeller University, the continual intake of fatty foods or fat-sugar combinations could reconfigure the hormonal system and predispose children to crave a fatty taste to achieve hormone balance. Stick to whole foods, in their natural state, as good choices for kids.*

The cocoa bean is now lauded for its healthful antioxidants while the addictive taste, aroma, and creamy consistency are ignored. While an ounce or two of chocolate may be considered a healthful snack, it's a risky one for persons with weak dopamine and/or opioid production. For persons declaring chocolate, or any food, as absolutely fabulous, indulge when you are with friends and don't bring it home!

Taste seems pretty predictable until something as simple as a middle-ear infection damages a part of the circuitry. Middle-ear infections afflict seventy-five percent of kids before the age of three. The infection can damage the nerve, chorda tympani, that carries taste information from the front of the tongue to the brain. The enjoyment of certain flavors is then limited, but the oral sensation of texture is intensified. In a similar fashion, damage to the glossopharnygeal nerve during removal of the adenoids and tonsils may lead to overeating.

Fatty food has a unique texture---creamy or oily. Taste impairment puts kids at increased risk of becoming obese as they are tempted by the texture of fat, especially a fat that melts in your mouth---chocolate.

Take Charge!
When it comes to consuming tempting foods, don't be a victim of your opioids. Think seldom.

Your insula interprets tempting

Taste alone does not determine the rating of a food. It's about flavor, the combination of taste, texture, and aroma. If the brain's interpretation of a food's flavor is "delicious," that food is elevated to a preferred status---tempting. The analysis takes place in the insula, where sensory stimuli, emotions, and bodily changes determine your feelings.

The amygdala---the central structure of an emotional response---is often called the *heart of an emotion*. It provides much of the sensory information about food to the insula.

THE COMPONENTS OF "AROMA"

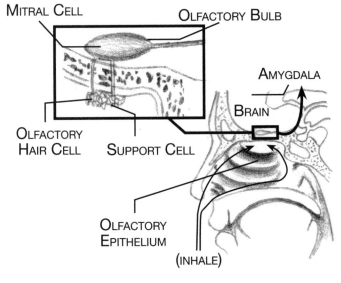

The amygdala connects with neurons that are specifically tuned to five types of oral stimuli: viscosity, grittiness, creamy texture, capsaicin (a hot sensation), and temperature. Information regarding the aroma of the food travels directly to the amygdala, quickly initiating desire or aversion. Your nose dominates the evaluation of a food.

The amygdala responds more vigorously to the emotional novelty of a food that is especially tasty or obnoxious. Add the adjective "new" to a food and you've captured the attention of your amygdala---a sampling is forthcoming.

Brain Analysis of "Tempting"

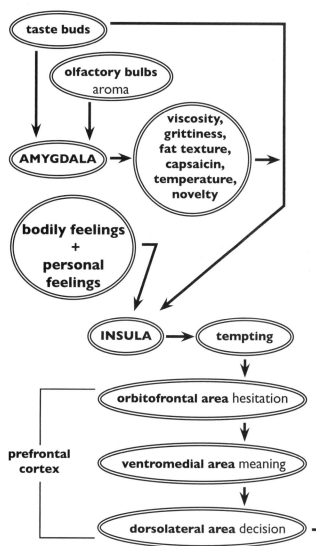

Once the insula rates a food as *tempting*, a signal proceeds from the insula to the executive area of the brain, the *prefrontal cortex*. "Prefrontal" means the most forward part of the brain, just behind and above the forehead. Your "cortex" is the outer layer of the brain.

The orbitofrontal area (the prefrontal cortex) acts to slow impulsive action, permitting cognitive evaluation and a thoughful plan. Because atrophy of the orbitofrontal cortex is related to gluttonous overeating, this area of the prefrontal cortex is, practically speaking, the location of *willpower*.

The first few bites of a tempting food are *out of this world*. As you continue to eat, the emotional drive to seek and eat the food may unconsciously diminish. The fabulous food could get downgraded to ordinary or possibly repulsive. In a process called *habituation*, you eventually lose the desire to eat the food at all---sometimes.

THE ON-OFF SWITCH

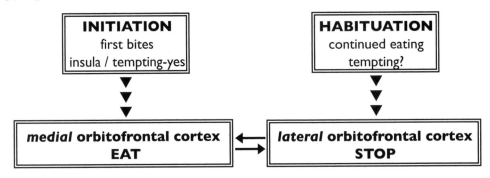

The orbitofrontal cortex plays an important role in habituation of tempting foods. Recent functional imaging studies suggest that the lateral and medial areas of the orbitofrontal cortex have opposing functions, similar to an on-off switch. The experience of hunger and motivation to eat is associated with the medial orbitofrontal cortex. Once both hunger and desire are satisfied, the activity switches to the lateral region. Habituation is not guaranteed, however. Your amygdala can interfere with the normal workings of the on-off switch when tempting foods light up the dopamine-producing reward circuit.

David Kessler, author of *The End of Overeating*, explains that functional MRIs of some individuals reveal the amygdalae, located in the right and left hemispheres of the brain, are hyperactivated by tempting foods. The excessive stimulation of the amygdalae can silence the body's homeostatic mechanisms that regulate food intake---no habituation.

These persons are especially vulnerable to overeating in the presence of tempting foods. They find it hard to resist fat, sugar, and/or salt, rarely feel satisfied eating healthful meals, and think about what to eat in the next meal while eating.

When the amygdala is hyperactivated, the reward circuit, normally disengaged as eating begins, remains active during the entire eating episode. You thus eat too much food, if you are one of these people. What can be done? Think! Practice *cognitive muscle training*, explained in this chapter, and do your homework at the end of the chapter: "Take Charge: A Ten-Step Program."

> **Take Charge!**
> *To make healthful foods your tempting foods,*
> *they must smell good, taste great, and be visually appealing.*

Why I Want to Eat What I Eat

The drive to eat is one of the most powerful urges of human behavior. Now match the basic passion to eat with an environment loaded with tempting foods, and you are faced with continual temptation.

Processing emotional information through cognitive structures is optional for the brain. In the absence of an alert prefrontal cortex, "wants" easily dominate behavior.

The work of Joseph LeDoux confirmed that the amygdala can excite an emotional response to a tempting food independent of cognitive input. LeDoux demonstrated the options available to the human brain using the analogy of a high-road and a low-road circuitry.

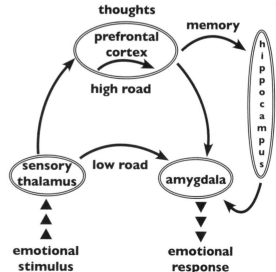

Before the prefrontal cortex can generate thoughts about a food, the amygdala can react to the stimulus. That's the low road. To think before eating a tempting food---that's the high road.

Loving a food is the first step to wanting it, an urge that can be totally unrelated to feeling full---but heightened by hunger. A practical suggestion: When you are mentally fatigued, avoid a conflict with your emotions. Your rational brain is likely to lose.

The Daily Dilemma
The tempting food I love is _____
                        Do you want the food now? yes or no
                        Will you seek the food now? yes or no

When a food is rated by the insula as tempting, the excitatory state of your amygdala determines the degree of desire to seek the food. The striatum elicits the "want" value of the food. The orbitofrontal cortex allows hesitation for the ventromedial cortex to add meaning and self-control. Lastly, the dorsolateral prefrontal cortex makes the decision.

Will your amygdala be energized to seek your tempting food right now? Look at the examples of factors contributing to seeking a tempting food in the diagram on page 33. Balancing these factors is important in managing temptation.

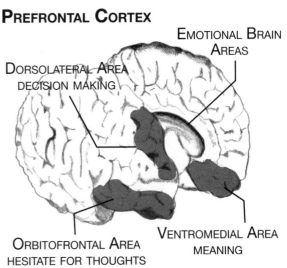

PREFRONTAL CORTEX

EMOTIONAL BRAIN AREAS

DORSOLATERAL AREA
DECISION MAKING

ORBITOFRONTAL AREA
HESITATE FOR THOUGHTS

VENTROMEDIAL AREA
MEANING

Will the striatum evaluate the tempting food as having sufficient desire to motivate a search? Notice the factors that will contribute to an energized striatum. Staying away from fast-food vendors is an easy way to limit these factors.

Will the orbitofrontal cortex inhibit the emotional drive sufficiently for self-control and a thoughtful decision about the tempting food? Your cognitive skills (cognitive muscle training) and other offensive strategies discussed in this chapter can be protective.

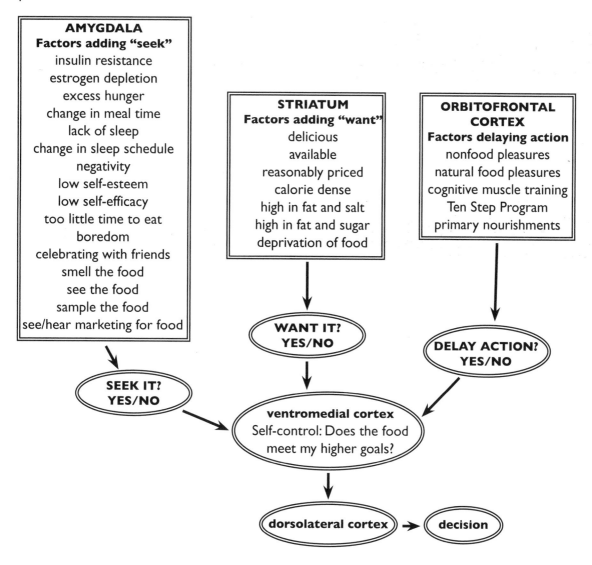

AMYGDALA
Factors adding "seek"
insulin resistance
estrogen depletion
excess hunger
change in meal time
lack of sleep
change in sleep schedule
negativity
low self-esteem
low self-efficacy
too little time to eat
boredom
celebrating with friends
smell the food
see the food
sample the food
see/hear marketing for food

STRIATUM
Factors adding "want"
delicious
available
reasonably priced
calorie dense
high in fat and salt
high in fat and sugar
deprivation of food

ORBITOFRONTAL CORTEX
Factors delaying action
nonfood pleasures
natural food pleasures
cognitive muscle training
Ten Step Program
primary nourishments

WANT IT?
YES/NO

DELAY ACTION?
YES/NO

SEEK IT?
YES/NO

ventromedial cortex
Self-control: Does the food meet my higher goals?

dorsolateral cortex → **decision**

Having passions in your life---other than your loved foods---adds offensive strategies against temptation: a personal list of passions other than tempting foods; an availability of natural foods you have learned to love; a checklist of primary nourishments. (Adapted from *Integrative Nutrition* by Joshua Rosenthal.)

Joshua Rosenthal, author of *Integrative Nutrition*, suggests that play, fun, touch, romance, intimacy, love, achievement, success, art, music, self-expression, leadership, excitement, adventure, and spirituality are primary nourishments. These delaying factors fulfill us physically, mentally, emotionally, and spiritually. Food becomes secondary nourishment.

Perhaps the tempting food will win, but your offensive strategies provide the chance to stop before consuming it, at least some of the time. Each successful intervention strengthens self-efficacy and self-esteem, making it easier to plan ahead and avert the temptation the next time.

Critter Diary

My current horse pal, Noah, has a weakness for sweets. He opened the refrigerator in the barn, pulled out the twenty-five-pound bag of carrots, tore open the plastic bag, and ate all the carrots. What amazed me was his desire for more carrots that same day. Perhaps he, too, has the hyperactivated amygdala Kessler describes.

When Food Cravings Win

Almost everyone deals with cravings for calorie-dense foods, according to S.K. Das and co-workers. They find that you can lose more weight by conceding to your cravings less frequently than by attempting total abstinence. In other words, don't be too hard on yourself.

Cognitive muscle training is a surrender to a tempting food *on your terms*. Each step is a thought process that deflects impulsivity and puts you in charge of the timing and the amount of a tempting food consumed.

Each experience is followed by charting your thoughts and feelings in a diary. Studies comparing persons following weight-management programs report that the process of recording your experiences with food seals success.

Cognitive muscle training I

Level one converts a craving into an objective, rational experience.

In level one, you evaluate only the hedonic value of the tempting food. Your emotional memory of the tempting food is influenced by a variety of perceptions and conditions surrounding consumption---hunger, mood, sleep status, stressors, exertion---not just the food.

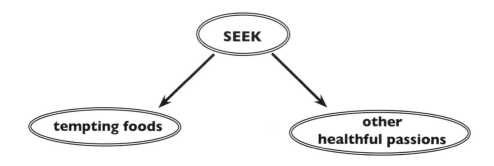

<u>Level One</u>

Cut the tempting food into small pieces. Before you begin eating, rate your love for the food from 1 to 10.

Eat slowly. Focus 100 percent of your attention on the food. Enjoy every bite. Silently evaluate the flavor, consistency, and other enjoyable traits of the food. After the last bite, rate your love for the food at that moment: 1 to 10.

Follow this protocol each time your craving wins. Record your thoughts and feelings in a diary along with the answers to these questions: Was the last bite as fabulous as the first and why did you eat the whole thing?

Meanwhile, keep developing other pleasures in your life. When you notice new passions substituting for tempting foods, or a tempting food not tasting as good as you imagined, you are ready to try the next level.

Cognitive muscle training II

Level two strengthens the power of your will (the orbitofrontal cortex) over a tempting food. Try versions A and B.

<u>Level Two A</u>

Goal: Become aware of any diminishing pleasure toward a tempting food and use the feeling as the cue to stop eating it.

Cut the food into small pieces. Before you begin eating, rate your love for the food from 1 to 10.

Rate how much you want the food at that moment from 1 to 10. Your desire for a tempting food should be less intense most of the time if you are developing other passions in your life.

Now focus 100 percent of your attention on the tempting food. Feel the pleasure as the food saturates your senses and notice any change in mood as you eat.

Ask yourself: Will I feel any better taking the next bite? When the answer is yes, take another bite and continue. When the answer is no, stop eating and immediately throw the rest of the food away.

Remember to record your experience and thoughts in a diary along with the answers to these questions: How many bites did you take and how can you improve?

Level Two B

Goal: Keep the brain actively engaged and in charge of what you eat.

Cut the food into small pieces. Before you begin eating, rate your love for the food from 1 to 10. Rate how much you want the food at that moment from 1 to 10. Your desire for a tempting food should be less intense most of the time if you are developing other passions in your life.

Now focus on the food and ask yourself: What taste makes this food irresistible? For example, if you love cherry pie, what's most tempting? Is it the crust, the cherries, or the ice cream on top? For chocolate chip cookies, is it the chips or the dough? Do you want the cake or just the frosting? For the big burger with bacon, cheese, and sauce on a bun, is it the bun, the burger, the burger with bacon? Take time to make a thoughtful decision.

Set aside the yummy stuff and throw the rest away. Focus 100 percent of your attention on eating the tempting portion of the food. Eat slowly and enjoy your experience.

Now get out a pen and record your thoughts and feelings about controlling the eating episode in a diary. Ask yourself if you could eat less of the irresistible portion next time.

Critter Diary

 As a young child I had no desire to eat, never felt hungry. If you are not hungry, then it seems the only reason to eat is pleasure. I chose fudge and buttered, salted popcorn as my diet. Combined with daily supplements I survived but carried the baggage of tempting foods into adulthood.

One day, I walked past an Old English sheep dog puppy snoozing in the window of the local animal shelter. She looked adorable! I asked if I could adopt the puppy. She had hip dysplasia at birth and the shelter staff was considering euthanasia.

Knowing nothing about the disease, I gladly took the pup home, named her Jennifer, and gave her daily doses of natural medicine--- lots of hugs. Jennifer lived just thirteen short years, but she brought a smile to anyone who glanced her way, especially when she jogged along the hiking trails, carrying water and snacks in a backpack. Her playful antics during our walks at the beach are particularly memorable. My favorite memory? The day she was chasing a wave and suddenly darted in front of a jogger intently racing through the sand. He tumbled over her furry frame, landed on his feet, and just kept on running.

Jennifer's sweetness brought more pleasure into my daily life than any amount of tempting food. In fact, tempting foods slowly fell lower and lower on my list of wants as I treasured her companionship more and more over the years. I still enjoy a piece of fudge or a warm chocolate chip cookie now and then. I still mentally score the treat and come to the same conclusion: It wasn't nearly as good as I had imagined. But my score for Jennifer is always the same. She was a perfect ten!

Tempting Foods: Are You Hooked?

Studies from the Monell Chemical Senses Center (www.monell.org) reveal that cravings for food are possibly the evolutionary basis of all craving behavior. Both addiction and obesity result from forage and ingestion, habits that persist despite possible catastrophic consequences. Looking at the response of the brain to reward, structures involved in drug cravings---such as the orbitofrontal cortex and striatum---are activated by tempting foods as well.

Not all humans exposed to drugs or junk food find them tempting. The increased availability of comfort foods and street drugs lures vulnerable individuals into obesity and/or drug addiction. There may also be gender differences, at least for food addiction.

Gene-Jack Wang taught a cognitive-inhibition technique to both men and women and then presented them with their favorite foods while brain scans were recorded. Only the men's brains demonstrated less active hunger signals and reward circuits. Nora Volkow, director of the National Institute of Drug Addiction, speculated that the female brain may be hardwired to eat whenever food is available because of her biological needs during pregnancy and lactation.

Can you become a chocoholic? More than three hundred substances have been identified in chocolate. The amount of each substance is too small to have any effect on appetite. Scientists do agree, however, that dependency on chocolate---or another food that you find addicting---is probably due to its taste, texture, and aroma, causing intense pleasure and a desire for more.

Can you be addicted to caffeine? Ninety percent of all adults in the United States consume caffeine daily. Caffeine in coffee, tea, soda, and medications can lead to physical dependency as the brain develops a tolerance to the chemical. The symptoms of withdrawal from caffeine begin shortly after you stop consuming it. Headaches, nausea, and sleepiness affect about one out of every two individuals. Unlike street drugs, caffeine increases the production of dopamine primarily in the prefrontal cortex and only weakly in the brain's reward circuit. You feel more alert than elated. Thus most scientists don't categorize caffeine as a true addiction.

EXPOSURE TO SUGAR

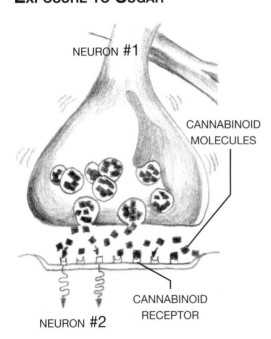

NEURON #1

CANNABINOID MOLECULES

CANNABINOID RECEPTOR

NEURON #2

Can you get hooked on sweets? There are lots of people who have cravings to overeat sweets and feel better when they indulge. Although doughnuts are not in the same category as addictive drugs, studies of heroin (enhancing opioids) and marijuana (releasing cannabinoids) are clues that an overlap may exist between sweets and drugs. Block the cannabinoid receptors with medication and you can cut in half the consumption of sweets.

Critter Diary

Meet the sisters, Belle and Starr. Working most of their lives on an Amish farm, these draft horses are a team, pulling wagons, plows, and carriages. Since they weigh more than a ton each, it seemed almost humorous to see them run away from an apple.

There is a rationale for their fear. Belle and Starr have shy, gentle temperaments. Their natural timidity sets them into a gallop, away from any novel object. Trained for work, these animals were well fed, but treats were never offered. You can't love something you have never tasted.

Belle and Starr have now tasted apples, l-o-v-e them, and want them! Each time they run toward me for a bite of apple, I am reminded of how rewarding real food can be---no pie crust around it, no ice cream on top, just a plain apple.

Conclusion

Seeking is a highly efficient emotional response, effectively networked throughout the brain. Take charge: Empower your intellect. Develop more cognitive muscle and follow the Ten-Step Program outlined in the homework section.

Before you begin the homework, jot down your tempting foods. Then rate them (1 to 10) for the "want it" value. Lastly, estimate how often you are tempted by the food.

PERSONAL PRIORITIES

Date:_____ Tempting foods	"Want" Rating (1-10)	# of temptations per day or week

The Starting Point: Tackle the food with the lowest rating and frequency. Accumulate success using the Ten-Step Program. And if the tempting food wins, practice Cognitive Muscle Training as outlined in the text.

Brain Homework: Nutrition for a Hungry Brain
Take Charge: A Ten-Step Program

The philosophy of the steps: *Keep your brain balanced and tempting foods can't control your life.* Place a (check) next to the steps you have incorporated into your lifestyle.

Step One: Admit that you have lost control over tempting foods. (   )

From this moment forward YOU will decide when a tempting food is consumed and how much you will eat. That glob of fat/sugar or fat/salt rules your life no more. You are taking charge.

Step Two: Avoid hunger by maintaining a rhythm to your meals. (   )

Hunger puts you at great risk for food cravings. Eat four small meals at planned times. Include a small portion of protein to aid in satiety, and a piece of fruit to curb the desire for a dessert.

Step Three: Eight is the magic number for sleep. (   )

Sleep deprivation, second only to hunger, increases the desire to find a tempting food and eat insatiably. Add sleep to your rhythmic plan for meals.

Step Four: Put your day on cruise control. (   )

Stress leads you to comfort foods. Boredom promotes eating to pass time. Too much to do or nothing to do can trigger a longing for a tasty food. Alternate mental activity with physical activity throughout the day to keep the mind balanced.

Step Five: Bond with a buddy. (   )

A buddy is a person who has struggled with tempting foods and weight gain. This person knows the difficulties you face and is willing to be there for you when temptation calls. One buddy or a buddy club of several interactive persons is indispensable to your success.

Step Six: Eat before you party with friends. (   )

It's great to be with friends, but when combined with eating---beware. Your opioid response to friends sets up a desire to keep the good times rolling with food, alcohol, and desserts. Have a snack before the party and sip a glass of water as you enjoy socializing. Plan how much alcohol you will drink beforehand and stick to your commitment. Then, overindulge in laughter.

Step Seven: Be prepared for unplanned temptations. (   )

The brain instinctually activates the reward circuit when tempting foods are within view, are calorie dense, are familiar to your taste buds, or offer variety. Protect yourself by carrying gum for times of temptation. Chewing decreases appetite and caloric intake. Additionally, keep a small sack of nuts and small pieces of dried fruit handy for those unplanned moments of true hunger. Floss and brush your teeth often. Consult a dental professional regarding your eating habits.

Step Eight: Act on sadness before tempting food becomes the remedy. (   )

When you feel sad or lonely, your brain begins searching for ways to feel good. Get up and actively help others who are sad or lonely. Visit someone in a nursing home, help a neighbor, or go to the animal shelter and volunteer your services. You get the idea.

Step Nine: Quiet your emotional brain every day. (   )

Sit down for two minutes each morning, close your eyes, listen to your breathing, and think *life is good, with or without tempting foods*. Gradually increase the total number of minutes to twenty each day.

Step Ten: Develop healthful, nonfood passions in your life. (   )

If food is your only passion in life, it will be difficult to avoid culinary temptations. Every brain searches for pleasure. Avoidance works for a short time. Then a flood of desire leads to overindulgence. Food is an active passion. You search, you cook, you chew, you swallow. Find healthful, active passions, things that bring you pleasure, or be ruled by your hungry brain.

Final thoughts: Are you taking charge of tempting foods? Review your list of Personal Priorities. Has your rating to want a tempting food diminished? Are you less tempted most of the time? Reward yourself---healthfully---for any improvements.

Key References

Abizaid, Alfonso, et al. Ghrelin Modulates the Activity and Synaptic Input Organization of Midbrain Dopamine Neurons while Promoting Appetite. *Journal of Clinical Investigation* 2006; 116(12):3229-3239.

Accolla, Riccardo, et al. Differential Spatial Representation of Taste Modalities in the Rat Gustatory Cortex. *Journal of Neuroscience* 2007; 27(6):1396-1404.

American Psychological Association. A Recipe for Overeating: Studies Outline Dangers of Mixing Stress, Deprivation and Tempting Foods. http://www.apa.org/releases/overeat (accessed 1/25/09).

Aunger, Robert. What's Special about HumanTechnology. *Cambridge Journal of Economics* 2009; 10.1093/cje/bep018.

Balleine, Bernard W. Neural Bases of Food-seeking: Affect, Arousal and Reward in Corticostriatolimbic Circuits. *Physiology & Behavior* 2005; 86:717-730.

Bartoshuk, Linda M., et al. Psychophysics of Sweet and Fat Perception in Obesity: Problems, Solutions and New Perspectives. *Philosophical Transactions of the Royal Society B: Biological Sciences* 2006; 361(1471):1137-1148.

Bender, G., et al. Neural Correlates of Evaluative Compared with Passive Tasting. *European Journal of Neuroscience* 2009; 30(2):327-338.

Berlin, Heather A., et al. Borderline Personality Disorder, Impulsivity, and the Orbitofrontal Cortex. *American Journal of Psychiatry* 2005; 162:2360-2373.

Bodenios, J.S., et al. Vagus Nerve Stimulation Acutely Alters Food Craving in Adults with Depression. *Appetite* 2007; 48(2):145-153.

Chambers, E. S. et al. Carbohydrate Sensing in the Human Mouth: Effects on Exercise Performance and Brain Activity. *Journal of Physiology* 2009; 587:1779-1794.

Christakis, Nicholas A., and James H. Fowler. The Spread of Obesity in a Large Social Network over 32 Years. *New England Journal of Medicine* 2007; 357:370-379.

Crerand, Candice E., et al. Changes in Obesity-related Attitudes in Women Seeking Weight Reduction. *Obesity* 2007; 15:740-747.

Das, S.K., et al. Low or Moderate Dietary Energy Restriction for Long-term Weight Loss: What Works Best? *Obesity* 2009; 17(11):2019-2024.

de Kloet, Annette, E., and Stephen C. Woods. Endocannabinoids and Their Receptors as Targets for Obesity Therapy. *Endocrinology* 2009; 150:2531-2536.

Del Parigi, Angelo, et al. Are We Addicted to Food? *Obesity Research* 2003; 11:493-495.

Dupertuis, Y. M., et al. Advancing from Immunonutrition to a Pharmaconutrition: A Gigantic Challenge. *Current Opinions in Clinical Nutrition and Metabolic Care* 2009; 12(4):398-403.

Figlewicz, Dianne P. Adiposity Signals and Food Reward: Expanding the CNS Roles of Insulin and Leptin. *American Journal of Physiology - Regulatory, Integrative, and Comparative Physiology* 2003; 284(4):R882-R892.

Finlayson, Graham, et al. Is It Possible to Dissociate 'Liking' and 'Wanting' for Foods in Humans? A Novel Experimental Procedure. *Physiology & Behavior* 2007; 90:36-42.

Frank, G.K., et al. Sucrose Activates Human Taste Pathways Differently from Artificial Sweetener. *Neuroimage* 2008; 39(4):1559-69.

Gailliot, Matthew T., and Roy F. Baumeister. The Physiology of Willpower: Linking Blood Glucose to Self-control. *Personality and Social Psychology Review* 2007; 11(4):303-327.

Gilhooly, C.H., et al. Food Cravings and Energy Regulation: The Characteristics of Craved Foods and Their Relationship with Eating Behaviors and Weight Change during 6 Months of Dietary Energy Restriction. *International Journal of Obesity* 2007; 31:1849-1858.

Grabenhorst, Fabian, et al. How Cognition Modulates Affective Responses to Taste and Flavor: Top-down Influences on the Orbitofrontal and Pregenual Cingulate Cortices. *Cerebral Cortex* 2008; 18:1549-1559.

Guijarro, A., et al. Hypothalamic Integration of Immune Function and Metabolism. *Progress in Brain Research* 2006; 153:367-405.

Hare, Todd A., et al. Self-control in Decision-making Involves Modulation of the vmPFC Valuation System. *Science* 2009; 324(5927):646-648.

Hetherington, Marion M., and Emma Boyland. Short-term Effects of Chewing Gum on Snack Intake and Appetite. *Appetite* 2007; 48:397-401.

Key References (cont'd)

Hollis, J.F., et al. Weight Loss during the Intensive Intervention Phase of the Weight-loss Maintenance Trial. *American Journal of Preventive Medicine* 2008; 35(2):118-126.

Isganaitis, Elvira, and Robert H. Lustig. Fast Food, Central Nervous System Insulin Resistance, and Obesity. *Arteriosclerosis, Thrombosis, and Vascular Biology* 2005; 25:2451-2462.

Jackson, Mark E., and Bita Moghaddam. Amygdala Regulation of Nucleus Accumbens Dopamine Output Is Governed by the Prefrontal Cortex. *Journal of Neuroscience* 2001; 21:676.

James, G. A., et al. Prolonged Insula Activation during Perception of Aftertaste. *Neuroreport* 2009; 20(3):245-250.

Kadohisa, M., et al. The Primate Amygdala: Neuronal Representations of the Viscosity, Fat Texture, Temperature, Grittiness and Taste of Foods. *Neuroscience* 2005; 132:33-48.

Kalivas, Peter W. Glutamate Systems in Cocaine Addiction. *Current Opinion in Pharmacology* 2004; 4(1):23-29.

Killgore, William D.S., and Deborah A. Yurgelun-Todd. Affect Modulates Appetite-related Brain Activity to Images of Food. *International Journal of Eating Disorders* 2006; 39:357-363.

Leibowitz, S. F., et. al. Puberty Onset in Female Rats: Relationship with Fat Intake, Ovarian Steroids, and the Peptides, Galanin and Enkephalin, in the Paraventricular and Medial Preoptic Nuclei. *Journal of Neuroendocrinology* 2009; 21(6):538-549.

Lerner, Alicia, et al. Involvement of Insula and Cingulate Cortices in Control and Suppression of Natural Urges. *Cerebral Cortex* 2009; 19:218-223.

Lingford-Hughes, Anne, and David Nutt. Neurobiology of Addiction and Implications for Treatment. *British Journal of Psychiatry* 2003; 182:97-100.

Macht, Michael, et al. Emotions and Eating in Everyday Life: Application of the Experience-Sampling Method. *Ecology of Food and Nutrition* 2004; 43(4):11-21.

Mattes, R.D. The Taste of Fat Elevates Postprandial Triacylglycerol. *Physiology & Behavior* 2001; 74:343-348.

Mattes, Richard D., and Barry M. Popkin. Nonnutritive Sweetener Consumption in Humans: Effects on Appetite and Food Intake and Their Putative Mechanisms. *Physiology & Behavior* 2001; 74:343-348.

McCaffery, Jeanne M., et al. Differential Functional Magnetic Resonance Imaging Response to Food Pictures in Successful Weight-loss Maintainers Relative to Normal-weight and Obese Controls. *American Journal of Clinical Nutrition* 2009; 90(4):928-934.

Meguid, Michael M., et al. Hypothalamic Dopamine and Serotonin in the Regulation of Food Intake. *Nutrition* 2000; 16:843-857.

Mela, David J. Eating for Pleasure or Just Wanting to Eat? Reconsidering Sensory Hedonic Responses as a Driver of Obesity. *Appetite* 2006; 47:10-17.

Moayedi, Massieh, and Irit Weissman-Fogel. Is the Insula the "How Much" Intensity Coder? Journal of *Neurophysiology* 2009; 102:1345-1347.

Monell Chemical Senses Center. Images of Desire: Brain Regions Activated by Food Craving Overlap with Areas Implicated in Drug Craving. http://www.sciencedaily.com (released 8-11-09).

Nestler, Eric J. Historical Review: Molecular and Cellular Mechanisms of Opiate and Cocaine Addiction. *Trends in Pharmacological Sciences* 2004; 25(4):210-218.

Newcombe, Rachel. Is Junk Food Addictive? http://www.bupa.co.uk/health_information/html/health_news (released 7/19/09).

Onoda, Keiko, et al. Laterality of Human Primary Gustatory Cortex Studied by MEG. *Chemical Senses* 2005; 30:657-666.

Pacher, Pal, et al. The Endocannabinoid System as an Emerging Target of Pharmacotherapy. *Pharmacological Reviews* 2006; 58:389-462.

Pagotto, Uberto, et al. The Endocannabinoid System and the Treatment of Obesity. *Annals of Medicine* 2005; 37:270-275.

Piech, Richard M. Neural Correlates of Affective Influence on Choice. *Brain and Cognition* 2010; 72(2):282-288.

Rogers, Peter J., and Hendrik J. Smit. Food Craving and Food "Addiction": A Critical Review of the Evidence from a Biopsychosocial Perspective. *Pharmacology Biochemistry and Behavior* 2000; 66(1):3-14.

Key References (cont'd)

Rolls, E.T. Functions of the Orbitofrontal and Pregenual Cingulate Cortex in Taste, Olfaction, Appetite and Emotion. *Acta Physiologica Hungarica* 2008; 95(2):131-164.

Rolls, Edmund T. Brain Mechanisms Underlying Flavour and Appetite. *Philosophical Transactions of the Royal Society B: Biological Sciences* 2006; 361(1471):1123-1136.

_____. Functional Neuroimaging of Umami Taste: What Makes Umami Pleasant? *American Journal of Clinical Nutrition* 2009; 90:804S-813S.

_____. Taste, Olfactory, and Food Texture Processing in the Brain, and the Control of Food Intake. *Physiology and Behavior* 2005; 85(1):45-56.

Science and Nature: Human Body & Mind. Science of Supertasters. http://www.bbc.co.uk/science/humanbody (accessed 9/5/09).

Sipe, Daniel. Social Gastronomy: Fourier and Brillat-Savarin. *French Cultural Studies* 2009; 20:219-236.

Smith, Gerard P., and Graham J. Dockray. Introduction to the Reviews on Appetite. *Philosophical Transactions of the Royal Society B*. FirstCite e-publishing (accessed 11/5/09).

Society for Neuroscience. Appetite and Food Intake. http://web.sfn.org (accessed 11/15/08).

_____. Smell and the Olfactory System. http://www.sfn.org (accessed 11/5/08).

_____. Taste Detectors. http://www.sfn. org (accessed 11/5/08).

_____. Taste Intensity. http://www.sfn. org (accessed 11/5/08).

Taber, Katherine H., and Robin A. Hurley. Endocannabinoids: Stress, Anxiety, and Fear. *Journal of Neuropsychiatry & Clinical Neurosciences* 2009; 21:2.

Van Leijenhorst, Linda, et al. What Motivates the Adolescent? Brain Regions Mediating Reward Sensitivity across Adolescence. *Cerebral Cortex* 2010; 20:61-69.

Veldhuizen, Maria G., et al. Trying to Detect Taste in a Tasteless Solution: Modulation of Early Gustatory Cortex by Attention to Taste. *Chemical Senses* 2007; 32(6):569-581.

Volkow, Nora D., and Roy A. Wise. How Can Drug Addiction Help Us Understand Obesity? *Nature Neuroscience* 2005; 8(5):555-560.

Von Dem Hagen, Elisabeth A. H., et al. Leaving a Bad Taste in Your Mouth but Not in My Insula. *Social Cognitive and Affective Neuroscience* 2009; 4:379-386.

Wang, Gene-Jack, et al. Evidence of Gender Differences in the Ability to Inhibit Brain Activation Elicited by Food Stimulation. *Proceedings of the National Academy of Sciences* 2009; 106:1249-1254.

Wang, Gene-Jack, et al. Exposure to Appetitive Food Stimuli Markedly Activates the Human Brain. *NeuroImage* 2004; 21:1790-1797.

Wang, Gene-Jack, et al. Gastric Stimulation in Obese Subjects Activates the Hippocampus and Other Regions Involved in Brain Reward Circuitry. *Proceedings of the National Academy of Sciences* 2006; 103(42):15641-15645.

Waterhouse, Jim, et al. Food Intake in Healthy Young Adults: Effects of Time Pressure and Social Factors. *Chronobiology International* 2005; 22(6):1069-1092.

Wenner, Melinda. The Obesity-earache Link. *Scientific American Mind*, December 2008/January 2009, p. 14.

Wijga, Alet H., et al. Adenotonsillectomy and the Development of Overweight. *Pediatrics* 2009;123(4):1095-1101.

Wise, Roy A. Role of Brain Dopamine in Food Reward and Reinforcement. *Philosophical Transactions of the Royal Society B: Biological Sciences* 2006; 361(1471):1149-1158.

Woolley, J.D., et al. Binge Eating Is Associated with Right Orbitofrontal-insular-striatal Atrophy in Frontotemporal Dementia. *Neurology* 2007; 69:1424-1433.

Yoshida, Ryusuke, et al. Endocannabinoids Selectively Enhance Sweet Taste. *Proceedings of the National Academy of Sciences* 2010; 107:935-939.

Zickler, Patrick. Nicotine Withdrawal Linked to Disrupted Glutamate Signaling. *NIDA Notes* 2005; 19(6).

Zink, C.F., et al. Human Striatal Activation Reflects Degree of Stimulus Saliency. *Neuroimage* 2006; 29(3):977-83.

Following Chapter Five, "Resources" lists current books that may be referenced in this chapter.

THE BRAIN

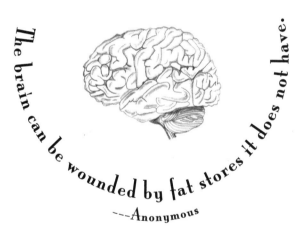

The brain can be wounded by fat stores it does not have.

---Anonymous

Chapter Two
Calories: Obesity and the Altered Brain

Fire within Fat Cells 52

The Stressed Fat Cell 55

Body Fat Facts 57
    Beneficial brown fat 57
    White fat warning 57

Beyond Insulin Resistance 60

The Inflamed Brain 63
    Inflammaging 63
    Adipositis 64
    Medication 67

Harnessing Sirtuins 68

Conclusion 69

Brain Homework: Nutrition for a Hungry Brain
    Two Basic Steps 70

Key References 74

*A little knowledge that acts
is worth infinitely more
than much knowledge that is idle.*

---John Quincy Adams

Fire within Fat Cells

At least four hundred million persons worldwide are obese. Twenty million children under the age of five years are overweight. The numbers are expanding with the waistlines. In an environment where junk food is a meal, the theoretical possibility that obesity and malnutrition could exist in the same person is now fact. Alarming!

The last two decades have produced the most shocking rise in obesity in recorded history. Genes don't change in twenty years, but gene expression is altered anytime. In a fat-toxic environment, it's not just your body that suffers. Obesity is unhealthy for your brain, beginning with depression---and that's just the tip of the iceberg.

What's under that visible portion of the obesity iceberg? Lots of surprises. Recent discoveries have revised the concept that fat cells are simply storage depots for fuel. Adipose tissue is an *endocrine organ*. In plain English, your fat cells release an array of hormones that affect major metabolic processes. Sounds serious and it is.

Obesity is not just a physical problem.
It's an all-inclusive disorder
that has been linked to
fifty-five different medical complications,
including many affecting the brain.

---Lee M. Kaplan

Critter Diary

The front page of a national newspaper recently printed a comparison of money spent on pets by their loving guardians. Rating higher than pet toys, pet clothing, or diamond-studded collars, pet snacks and treats head the list. Even horses are reaping the "benefits" of human care. Feed stores sell big plastic containers shaped like apples. The container is designed to hang near the horse so you can provide treats anytime. The first ingredient in the apple treat is not apple, it's molasses.

Hand in hand with the emphasis on pet junk food is a growing list of diseases diagnosed in pets, beginning with obesity and followed by type-2 diabetes, cardiovascular disease, cancer, serious asthma, and inflamed joints. Obese animals are vulnerable to dementia as well.

What's happening to companion animals? No more famines and little need for physical work. The animal is exposed to a constant state of feasting, with no need to hunt for food, find shelter, or fight for survival. Does the scenario sound familiar?

Notice my miniature burro Angel basking in the sun. She's not pregnant, just too fat. She eats like a horse, literally. Raised by my horse Noah, they graze together all day long. Angel's metabolism is much more efficient than Noah's. She gets very fat, very fast. Angel now spends a portion of her day away from the green pasture on a time-out from eating. Full-grown, Angel will work pulling a small cart for cleanup around the farm. Like all of us, she needs to work.

Fat cells don't exist in the brain, but they can destroy your brain at a distance. What is the linkage between obesity and dementia? *Inflammation*. The capacity to localize an inflammatory response is a crucial step in the elimination of pathogens and in healing tissue. Local inflammatory events (redness, heat, swelling, pain) and systemic immune responses are coordinated to meet the challenge.

Cytokines are protein messengers released by specific immune cells---macrophage, T-cells, and B-cells. They act as cell-to-cell signals to initiate, enhance, or terminate inflammation. The cytokine pertinent to the discussion of obesity is *tissue necrosis factor-alpha*. Tissue necrosis factor-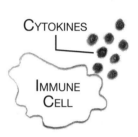alpha initiates inflammation in the body and brain. It increases liver production of *C-reactive protein*, a systemic marker of inflammation.

Unlike the obvious tissue damage caused by serious inflammatory diseases, mild, but chronic, inflammation is silently destructive over decades. Cholesterol accumulates in inflamed arteries, increasing the risk of heart attacks and strokes. The mutation of genes by inflammation may eventually initiate cancer. Insulin malfunctions in the presence of mild, chronic inflammation, increasing the risk of type-2 diabetes. Cognitive functions decline, as neurons atrophy under the constant presence of mild inflammation.

Surprisingly, your adipocytes (fat cells) can mimic immune cells and be a causal agent of inflammation. Chronically enlarged adipocytes produce inflammatory proteins called *adipocytokines*, identical to the cytokines released by immune cells.

With an epidemic of obesity in both children and adults, the inflammation generated by adipose tissue has become one of the most intriguing areas of investigation. Scientists need to find the tools to put out the fire generated within overstuffed adiopocytes and convince the world that prevention of obesity is good for the brain.

The Stressed Fat Cell

STRESS RESPONSE

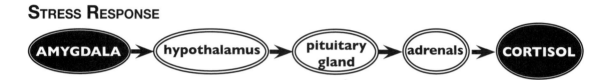

Stress is an emotion existing in the mind, not in your fat cells. It is triggered by the amygdala and driven by the hormone cortisol. How, then, does the expanding adipocyte become chronically stressed and spark an internal fire known as inflammation? The stressor is chemical, a state of physical decay.

Surplus energy stored within enlarged adipocytes causes significant oxidation (decay) to various structures within the cell. Within the neuron and other brain cells, the *endoplasmic reticulum* and the *mitochondria* demonstrate the greatest wear.

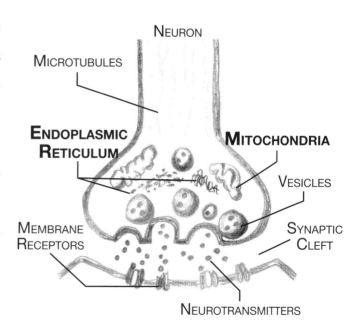

The endoplasmic reticulum is a continuous, folded, ribbon-like structure throughout a cell. Attached to the structure are enzymes spurring the chemical reactions essential to cellular metabolism. Continued excess fat accumulation in the adipocyte causes physiological stress within the cell---*oxidative stress*. Subjected to continual oxidative stress, the endoplasmic reticulum unfolds and inflammation follows, as the material is degraded and removed.

Availability of fuel is a cell's first priority. Mitochondria utilize oxygen and produce fuel for every metabolic activity within a cell. Of all cellular components, these fuel-burning structures are the most sensitive to the mushrooming oxidative stress within enlarged adipocytes.

When energy metabolism in the mitochondria is compromised by oxidation, survival mechanisms ensue. Signals are sent to the nucleus of the cell, awakening genes that synthesize a flood of antioxidant enzymes to neutralize oxidative stress. If obesity continues for long periods of time and the oxidation in mitochondria is not resolved, a new gene product is synthesized as a second line of defense.

The adipocyte begins to exude a glue on its surface called *macrophage adhesion protein*. A macrophage attaches to the adhesion protein on the adipocytes, is drawn within the cell, and begins secreting a range of inflammatory cytokines. The enlarged adipocytes are now dysfunctional. Each day you live in a state of obesity, cytokines generated by adipose tissue are released into the blood and contribute to dementia and other diseases.

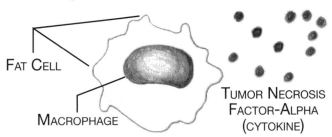

FAT CELL

MACROPHAGE

TUMOR NECROSIS FACTOR-ALPHA (CYTOKINE)

Body Fat Facts

There are two kinds of adipocytes, brown and white. The color of these fat cells is just one of their distinguishing traits.

Beneficial brown fat

Brown adipose tissue specializes in heat production to elevate core body temperature. An abundance of brown fat in newborns is critical. Without it, the baby cannot shiver to stay warm.

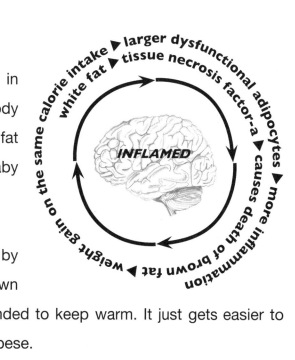

The inflammatory factor produced by enlarged white fat cells destroys brown fat, eliminating calories normally expended to keep warm. It just gets easier to gain weight when you are chronically obese.

White fat warning

There are two major white fat storage areas: subcutaneous fat, located between the skin and muscle; and visceral fat, localized under the stomach muscles. As you age, fat infiltrates the liver, bone marrow, and the abdominal cavity (visceral cavity). Visceral fat is busy pumping out a slew of inflammatory cytokines---tissue necrosis factor-alpha and others. Cytokine expression is tenfold higher in obese individuals with excess belly fat than in lean persons. Excess belly fat is nothing but trouble for your brain.

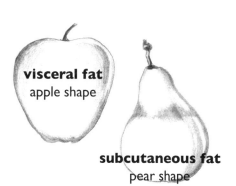

visceral fat
apple shape

subcutaneous fat
pear shape

Think about it!
*Liposuction removes only subcutaneous belly fat.
It's the visceral fat that causes the greatest harm to body and brain.*

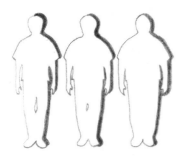

Visceral adipocytes have more receptors for the hormone cortisol than do subcutaneous adipocytes. A continual elevation of blood cortisol---noted in chronic obesity---spurs appetite and a series of metabolic alterations that add significant risk of disease, as shown in the diagram.

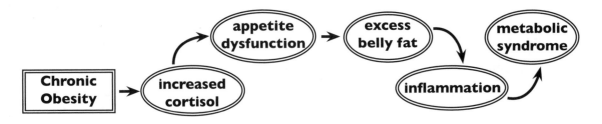

Both testosterone and cortisol receptors are concentrated in the viscera, contributing to an expanding waistline when too many calories are consumed. Men thus deposit more fat in the abdomen than premenopausal women.

After menopause, women express more testosterone than estrogen and store fat in the belly if overeating is the norm. Add chronic stress to the scenario, and the belly explodes in both genders.

What's the Point?
When the diet is high in fat, adipocytes within coronary vascular tissue exhibit a heightened pro-inflammatory state greater than that of visceral adipocytes.
Combine poor circulation with a very high fat meal and you could trigger a heart attack or a stroke.

How do you lose visceral fat? There is no way to target belly fat when losing weight. Sit-ups, crunches, and other exercises can strengthen abdominal muscles, but they don't melt belly fat preferentially. However, a greater loss of visceral fat is observed when moderate-to-intense aerobic exercise is combined with consuming fewer calories than when you just eat less food.

Critter Diary

When I adopted Salty, he weighed seventy-five pounds. For a German shepherd, his weight was within normal range. Because Salty's world to that point (six years) was garage bound, his muscles were poorly developed. Living in a rural environment, I was hopeful his new, active life would build enough muscle to support an osteoporotic right hip.

 As Salty's guardian, I wanted to make up for those lost six years he lived in a garage. I lavished him with the best food and organic chew bones for his teeth. Over the next year, my friends noted how good he looked. By the second year, comments had a darker tone. He looked big. Still, the thought of Salty being fat never crossed my mind.

The degenerated hip began to affect Salty's gait. I visited the veterinarian for an evaluation regarding a possible hip replacement. The doctor weighed Salty. He weighed one hundred two pounds. I assured the doctor he had gained muscle, but his glare of disbelief was telling. So I walked over to pinch Salty's subcutaneous fat, hoping to prove my point. There was nothing more to say. Salty's fat-fold was about two inches thick. He was not just fat, but morbidly obese. With the weight he carried and the inflammation produced by obesity, his hip was strained and painful.

Salty and I got to work on the problem. It was time for smaller portions and increased exercise. Two years later, he had dropped twenty pounds, and the results were amazing. There was no sign of a limp in his gait, no hint of pain, just a happy dog---and a happy guardian, too.

Beyond Insulin Resistance

Metabolic processes and immune responses are inextricably linked in daily functions. The hormone insulin plays a key role in promoting the storage of fat in adipocytes.

Normal Metabolic Activity

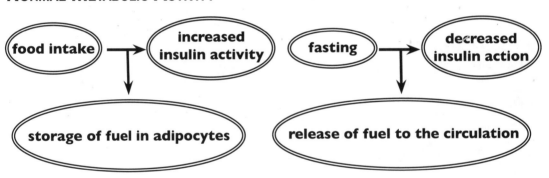

The immune cells rely upon fat stores as their fuel to mount an inflammatory response. To release the fat required for immune defense activities, insulin receptors on the adipocyte are blocked by the inflammatory cytokine, tissue necrosis factor-alpha. This metabolic state is called *insulin resistance*. Stored fat then flows into the circulation to fuel immune cells.

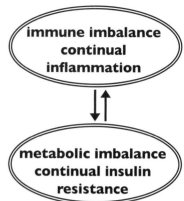

> ### *What's the Point?*
> *Geneticists believe that famine led to the selection of thrifty genes, predisposing individuals to insulin resistance. The brain, independent of insulin, then receives the bulk of available glucose during famine.*

Keeping in mind that acute inflammation is normally resolved in a few days, insulin resistance fits the temporary demands of an activated immune system. In persistent obesity, however, tissue necrosis factor-alpha is continually generated by adipose tissue. Insulin resistance then becomes a permanent metabolic state.

Although many inflammatory cytokines are expressed by the enlarged, macrophage-infiltrated fat cells, tissue necrosis factor-alpha is the most significant causal factor of insulin resistance. Like a fingerprint, the activity of this cytokine can be traced beyond chronic obesity and insulin resistance as causative in many diseases.

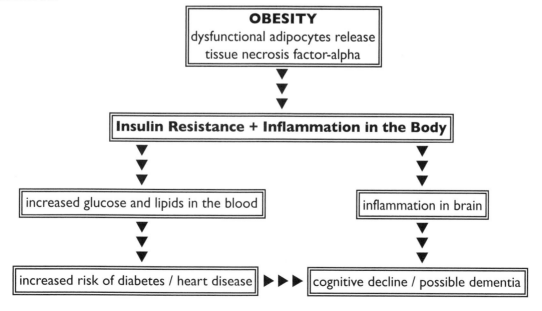

MORE
About obesity, insulin resistance, and life-threatening diseases

Look at the people around you. It won't be hard to find someone with lots of visceral fat. Their belly is bigger than their hips. Let's follow the cascade of biochemical events that might occur, silently, beginning with too much belly fat.

The visceral adipocytes flood the blood with tissue necrosis factor-alpha. As this inflammatory factor travels in the bloodstream, it reacts with insulin receptors on the surface of muscle, liver, and adipose cells. Steps in the insulin-signaling pathway are then disrupted, limiting the flow of glucose into cells---insulin resistance. Blood glucose rises above normal, and you have hyperglycemia and possibly type-2 diabetes.

Fat is metabolized into fuel only in the presence of sufficient carbohydrate in cells. The lack of adequate intracellular glucose slows the metabolism of fat in the muscle and liver. Lipid accumulates in these tissues and causes oxidative stress. The liver then releases C-reactive protein, the marker for mild, chronic inflammation in the body.

The inflammation increases the production of nitric oxide. Over time, the pancreas suffers under the toxic environment of excess nitric oxide. Insulin production falls, and the person diagnosed with type-2 diabetes is now confronted with pancreatic insufficiency and a daily need for insulin replacement.

Wait, that's not all the bad news. Hyperglycemia contributes to the oxidative stress within the adipocyte, accelerating the release of fatty acids in the blood. The individual now has hyperlipidemia, rapid narrowing of blood vessels, and the risk of hypertension. And the bad news continues.

Escalating body fat, mood disorders, poor memory processing, and cognitive decline---these conditions are ongoing in an inflammatory environment. Dementia is now a serious risk.

At this point, you should be getting the picture. Belly fat starts a domino effect of serious diseases.

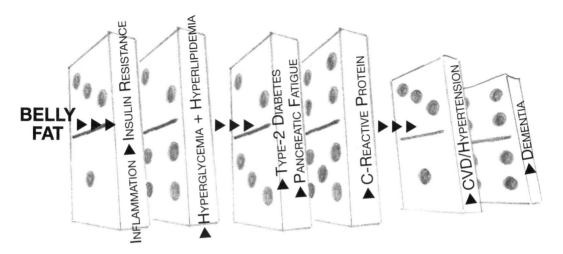

The Inflamed Brain
Alzheimer's is the fastest growing disease of late life.

---Deborah Gustafson

Aging poses the most significant risk for dementia. Why? *Inflammaging and adipositis.*

Inflammaging

Living longer is paralleled with an epidemic of chronic diseases. The term "inflammaging" has been coined to explain the age-dependent, up-regulation of the inflammatory response that contributes to diseases. What can happen to the aging brain? Inflammaging is solidly linked to cognitive decline and dementia. A test measuring levels of an inflammation marker---C-reactive protein---is used to determine neuroinflammation, even though C-reactive protein is not specific for the brain. It is a marker produced by the liver when inflammation is present in the body. More specific markers for brain inflammation are not yet available.

The cumulative activation of the immune system throughout life influences inflammaging. What factors have affected your blood level of C-reactive protein? Resolve to reduce your inflammatory boosters.

Checklist for Inflammaging	✔
Your infection history is related to serum levels of inflammatory proteins, measured as C-reactive protein. The greater the number of lifelong exposures to common pathogens, the higher the C-reactive protein.	
The presence of chronic inflammatory diseases, such as autoimmune disease, asthma, allergies, gingivitis, or periodontitis will positively affect C-reactive protein.	
Diseases causally related to inflammation, such as cardiovascular disease, insulin resistance, and type-2 diabetes, will elevate late-life C-reactive protein.	
Late-life inflammation, measured as C-reactive protein, is related to the excess of white fat tissue, especially belly fat. Chronically enlarged adipocytes produce inflammatory cytokines.	
Untreated mood disorders, such as depression and anxiety, trigger inflammation and the elevation of C-reactive protein.	
Poor-quality diet, lack of exercise, sleep deprivation, or life pressures (stressors) enhance cortisol release, inflammation, and C-reactive protein.	

Adipositis

Obesity is characterized by enlarged adipocytes. When adipocytes are enlarged and inflamed, infiltrated with macrophages, the condition is known as adipositis---regardless of age. There is remarkable diversity in the distribution of inflammation among various fat deposits and within the abdominal cavity. Overall, the current epidemic of obesity may be considered an inflammatory epidemic that predisposes to other forms of epidemic inflammation. Foods high in fat, as in tempting foods, have a significant correlation with adipositis. Right behind dietary fat as a risk for adipositis is sugar intake. Beyond their caloric densities, excess fat and sugar foster inflammation.

Are there data verifying the relationship of adipositis to cognitive decline and dementia? Since 2005, evidence has accumulated supporting the statement that elevated body mass index is associated with adverse neurocognitive outcomes. Middle-aged obese persons have decreased brain volume as compared to normal-weight persons. Looking at a range of ages from seventeen to seventy-nine, the brain scans of obese individuals show smaller whole brain and total gray matter volume than normal-weight and overweight persons.

In the largest evaluation of adipositis and memory, researchers at the Toulouse University School of Medicine in France investigated the relationship between body mass index and performance on tests of learning and remembering. More than 2000 men and women aged thirty-two to sixty-two were tested over a five-year period. Persons with the highest body mass index scored lowest on all cognitive tests and showed the greatest cognitive decline. N. D. Volkow and associates reported similar findings for persons in the United States.

While persons overweight in middle age
had a thirty-five percent increased risk of dementia,
obesity at mid-age increased the risk of dementia
by seventy-four percent.

---R. A. Whitmer

In a longitudinal study of 6,583 middle-aged persons by M. A. Beydoun and coworkers, abdominal circumferences were measured. Thirty-five years later, the incidence of dementia was significantly increased in persons who had central obesity in midlife, independent of diabetes or heart disease.

In 2009, a review of the literature summarized the findings regarding adiposity and dementia as follows:

- Excess belly fat at midlife is a predictor of dementia after age sixty-five.
- Waist circumference is a better predictor of dementia than body mass index.
- The parallel between adiposity and dementia is reduced in very elderly persons.
- Lower body mass index predicts dementia in frail, elderly people.
- Sudden, unexplained, rapid weight loss precedes dementia by decades.

Fifty percent of adults have too much belly fat. Even though fat stored under the skin is more widespread than visceral fat, the statistics for cognitive decline strongly favor deep abdominal fat. The true risk for dementia is determined by distinguishing between visceral and subcutaneous fat, according to J. A. Luchsinger and Deborah Gustafson. How can this recommendation be simply and reasonably implemented into the daily care of patients? There are no answers yet.

> **Think about it!**
> *Knowing that obesity is a modifiable risk for cognitive decline and dementia, will you take weight management seriously?*

The prevalence of severe childhood and adolescent adipositis in the United States has increased dramatically over the past three decades. The outcomes of early obesity now include hypertension, type-2 diabetes, lipid and liver abnormalities, sleep apnea, orthopedic problems, and depression. The current epidemic of pediatric obesity has resulted in great concern about the obese child's risk of dementia early in life.

Although the old scenario, *too much food and too little exercise*, is certainly relevant to obesity in all age groups, stress can also cause overweight children and adults to pack on pounds. According to Jason P. Block and colleagues, overweight persons who report psychosocial stress gain more weight than stressed persons with less body fat.

Chronic psychosocial stress suppresses a brain hormone, *brain-derived neurotrophic factor*, that dampens appetite. Stress can also cause damage (remodeling) in the hippocampus. In addition to processing perceptions into memory, the hippocampus is actively involved in the control of food intake. In fact,

a remodeled hippocampus may be, at least partially, at fault for eating too much and having poor recall of calories consumed. These behaviors are commonly noted among persons participating in weight management programs. Block's findings are reminders that stress threatens all Americans, especially those who are already overweight.

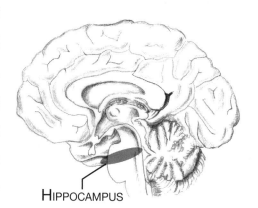

HIPPOCAMPUS

Medication

Nonsteroidal anti-inflammatory drugs are sold over the counter. They decrease the production of inflammatory cytokines in the brain and body. Can the use of these over-the-counter products lower the risk of dementia? The answer for baby aspirin is no. But what about much larger doses of the non-steroidal anti-inflammatory products? Can they protect the brain?

Some studies have suggested that persons taking anti-inflammatory medication may have less risk of dementia and Parkinson's disease. Still, how much do you take and when do you begin the preventive therapy? Most importantly, there are warnings of kidney failure and intestinal bleeding with decades of use. Researchers are hopeful that new, safer medications will soon be added to the arsenal of approaches against an inflamed brain. Meanwhile, chronic obesity and stress are significant determinants of inflammation that can be modified.

Harnessing Sirtuins

Certain genes, known as *sirtuins*, are silent information regulators. They are active when food intake is restricted. In a process similar to a 911 call of impending famine, the lack of calories sparks the expression of sirtuins to upgrade defenses against a stressor---in this case, famine.

Mice subjected to severe, lifelong caloric restriction certainly awaken their sirtuins. Glucose and insulin levels stabilize. Cells become better defended against the ravages of cellular aging. The brain releases growth factors that increase neuron differentiation from stem cells and improve neuron networking. Inflammatory cytokines, so damaging to neurons, are suppressed during the famine. The mice live three times longer. And it's good for humans, too, say researchers K. A. Varady and M. K. Hellerstein.

What about humans? Bronwen Martin and colleagues demonstrated that severe calorie restriction, but ample nutrient intake, improved learning and memory in women. The brain-derived growth factor measured in mice was released in the human brain as well.

Few persons of either sex are likely to choose severe calorie deprivation for a year, and certainly not for a lifetime. Fortunately, intermittent fasting may have a positive effect on your brain's growth factors, at least to some extent.

The next time you pig out on junk food or just eat too much food, remember the gene for sirtuin is sensitive to changes in the environment, such as feasting followed by famine. Consider a water or diluted-juice fast for a meal or two and follow up with healthful plant-based meals, high in antioxidants. Or simply extend the time interval between meals for beneficial effects on the brain, independent of cumulative calorie intake. The Homework at the end of this chapter will help you get started.

Conclusion

In closing this chapter, I want to remind readers who are lean that you too may suffer from an inflamed brain. Even in the absence of obesity, any chronic state of inflammation can lead to complications in the brain and cognitive decline. The nutrition guidelines presented in all the chapters are important, regardless of the fat mass below your chin.

Brain Homework: Nutrition for a Hungry Brain
Two Basic Steps

Step one: Think body fat

As you lose body fat, an important gene kicks into production, the gene that encodes *adiponectin*. Adiponectin is an anti-inflammatory cytokine secreted as you lose body fat. Adiponectin lowers the inflammatory protein, tissue necrosis factor-alpha, that stimulates insulin resistance. Start shrinking your fat cells today to regain insulin sensitivity---and more.

Guideline 1: Focus

Knowing how much belly fat you have is important. Measure your waist. Record the measurement. Compare monthly. Follow the nutrition homework, Guideline 2, to lose body fat.

MONTH	WAIST MEASUREMENT				
	YEAR 1	YEAR 2	YEAR 3	YEAR 4	YEAR 5
January					
February					
March					
April					
May					
June					
July					
August					
September					
October					
November					
December					

Guideline 2: Fasting

Successful, permanent fat loss requires self-efficacy, that is, a belief in yourself. Without confidence, you terminate the plan at the first incident of noncompliance. Self-efficacy can be acquired by creating experiences that are slightly difficult, yet attainable. Intermittent fasting has value for your psyche, the health of your brain, and the shrinkage of body fat.

K. A. Varady and M. K. Hellerstein studied intermittent fasting and reported increased activity of brain growth factors. Intermittent fasting also ignites sirtuin genes that defend against aging. Any successful fasting boosts efficacy and may improve the health span of your brain.

Consider a juice-fast day once a month. Dilute the juice of your choice one to one with water. Drink slowly as desired. Consult your doctor before attempting any fast.

RECORD OF FAST

Date	Food Consumed	Feelings/Notes

Why not drink plain water during a fast? A review by Matthew T. Gailliot and Roy F. Baumeister suggests that the amount of glucose in the blood is one important determinant of self-control. Fasting is energy-depleting for the brain. Failure is more likely when blood glucose is too low and the brain's appetite stimulants are triggered.

Step two: Think inflammation

If there is inflammation in your body, such as chronic obesity, there may be inflammation in your brain as well.

Guideline 1: C-reactive protein

The blood marker for inflammation is C-reactive protein. A person with excess fat in the abdomen, as compared to excess subcutaneous fat, has the highest value of this protein. Although your waist measurement is a crude guideline to C-reactive protein, you may prefer to have this value measured directly. Your physician can send a blood sample to a clinical laboratory for evaluation. The ideal value is less than 3.0.

How do you normalize C-reactive protein? "The most important thing is to lose excess body fat," says Michael Dansinger, a physician and scientist at the USDA Nutrition Research Center, Tufts University. He recommends a diet that has anti-inflammatory power. Of the four diets tested by Dansinger (Weight Watchers, The Zone, The Atkins, The Ornish Diet), the Ornish plan---a strict vegan diet---produced the best combined changes in body fat and C-reactive protein levels.

Guideline 2: Natural, naked food

Your eating habits can affect inflammation, beginning with too many calories. Plant foods have the lowest calorie value per unit weight. Only plant foods have antioxidants, natural chemicals that silence oxidative stress, the kindling for inflammation in your brain.

Eat a variety of plant foods in their natural state. Avoid juicing fruits and vegetables. Drink water when thirsty. Avoid pureed fruits and vegetables such as smoothies and pureed soups. Eat plant food as is, that is, raw, when possible. Use fresh or frozen varieties. Do not overcook vegetables.

Don't disguise plant food in fatty sauces, melted butter, or dressings; try a natural alternative. Season with lemon pepper or other herbs. Use fresh tomatoes or fresh salsa for added flavor. Try a dollop of nonfat cottage cheese on veggies.

Day	Natural, Naked Fruits and Vegetables Consumed
Mon.	
Tues.	
Wed.	
Thu.	
Fri.	
Sat.	
Sun.	

Key References

Alexandraki, Krystallenia, et al. Inflammatory Process in Type 2 Diabetes: The Role of Cytokines. *Annals of the New York Academy of Sciences* 2006; 1084:89-117.

Altman, Raul. Risk Factors in Coronary Atherosclerosis Athero-inflammation Meeting Point. *Thrombosis Journal* 2003; 1:4.

Andreasson, Anna, et al. A Putative Role for Cytokines in the Impaired Appetite in Depression. *Brain, Behavior, and Immunity* 2007; 21:147-152.

Atti, A.R., et al. Late-life Body Mass Index and Dementia Incidence: Nine-year Follow-up Data from the Kungsholmen Project. *Journal of the American Geriatrics Society* 2008; 56(1):111-116.

Badman, Michael K., and Jeffrey S. Flier. The Adipocyte as an Active Participant in Energy Balance and Metabolism. *Gastroenterology* 2007; 132(6):2103-2115.

Beydoun, M.A., et al. Obesity and Central Obesity as Risk Factors for Incident Dementia and Its Subtypes: A Systematic Review and Meta-analysis. *Obesity Reviews* 2008; 9(3):204-218.

Block, Jason P., et al. Psychosocial Stress and Change in Weight among U.S. Adults. *American Journal of Epidemiology* 2009; 170:181-192.

Breitner, J.C.S., et al. Risk of Dementia and Alzheimer's Disease with Prior Exposure to NSAIDS in an Elderly Community-based Cohort. *Neurology* 2009; 72:1899-1905.

Buchman, Aron S., et al. Physical Frailty in Older Persons Is Associated with Alzheimer Disease Pathology. *Neurology* 2008; 71:499-504.

Cereda, Emanuele, et al. Increased Visceral Adipose Tissue Rather than BMI as a Risk Factor for Dementia. *Age and Ageing* 2007; 36(5):488-491.

Chang, J., et al. Effect of Aging and Caloric Restriction on the Mitochondrial Proteome. *Journals of Gerontology Series A: Biological Sciences and Medical Sciences* 2007; 62:223-234.

Chatterjee, Tapan K., et al. Proinflammatory Phenotype of Perivascular Adipocytes: Influence of High-fat Feeding. *Circulation Research* 2009; 104:541-549.

Cournot, M., et al. Relation between Body Mass Index and Cognitive Function in Healthy Middle-aged Men and Women. *Neurology* 2006; 67:1208-1214.

Crerand, Canice E., et al. Changes in Obesity-related Attitudes in Women Seeking Weight Reduction. *Obesity* 2007; 15:740-747.

Dahl, Anna, et al. Being Overweight in Midlife is Associated with Lower Cognitive Ability and Steeper Cognitive Decline in Late Life. *Journals of Gerontology Series A: Biological Sciences and Medical Sciences* 2010; 65A(1):57-62.

Dansinger, Michael L., and Ernst J. Schaefer. Low-fat Diets and Weight Change. *Journal of the American Medical Association* 2006; 295:94-95.

Dansinger, Michael L., et al. Comparison of the Atkins, Ornish, Weight Watchers, and Zone Diets for Weight Loss and Heart Disease Risk Reduction. *Journal of the American Medical Association* 2005; 293:43-53.

Droge, W. Oxidative Aging and Insulin Receptor Signaling. *Journals of Gerontology Series A: Biological Sciences and Medical Sciences* 2005; 60:1378-1385.

Dupertuis, Y.M., et al. Advancing from Immunonutrition to a Pharmaconutrition: A Gigantic Challenge. *Current Opinions in Clinical Nutrition and Metabolic Care* 2009; 12(4):398-403.

Ebbeling, Cara, et al. Childhood Obesity: Public-health Crisis, Common Sense Cure. *Lancet* 2002; 360:473-782.

Epel, Elissa S., et al. Stress and Body Shape: Stress-induced Cortisol Secretion Is Consistently Greater among Women with Central Fat. *Psychosomatic Medicine* 2000; 62:623-632.

Fontana, L. Excessive Adiposity, Calorie Restriction, and Aging. *Journal of the American Medical Association* 2006; 295:1577-1578.

Key References (cont'd)

Fontana, Luigi, and Samuel Klein. Aging, Adiposity, and Calorie Restriction. *Journal of the American Medical Association* 2007; 297:986-994.

Furuhashi, M., et al. Adipocyte/Macrophage Fatty Acid-binding Proteins Contribute to Metabolic Deterioration through Actions in both Macrophages and Adipocytes in Mice. *Journal of Clinical Investigation* 2008; 118(7):2640-2650.

Furukawa, Shigetada, et al. Increased Oxidative Stress in Obesity and Its Impact on Metabolic Syndrome. *Journal of Clinical Investigation* 2004; 114:1752-1761.

Gailliot, Matthew T., and Roy F. Baumeister. The Physiology of Willpower: Linking Blood Glucose to Self-control. *Personality and Social Psychology Review* 2007; 11(4):303-327.

Galinier, Anne, et al. Adipose Tissue Proadipogenic Redox Changes in Obesity. *Journal of Biological Chemistry* 2006; 281(18):12682-12687.

Gorospe, Emmanuel C., and Jatin K. Dave. The Risk of Dementia with Increased Body Mass Index. *Age and Ageing* 2007; 36(1):23-29.

Gredilla, R., and G. Barja. Minireview: The Role of Oxidative Stress in Relation to Caloric Restriction and Longevity. *Endocrinology* 2005; 146:3713-3717.

Greenberg, Andrew S., and Martin S. Obin. Obesity and the Role of Adipose Tissue in Inflammation and Metabolism. *American Journal of Clinical Nutrition* 2006; 83(suppl):461S-465S.

Gregor, Margaret F., and Gokhan S. Hotamisligil. Adipocyte Stress: The Endoplasmic Reticulum and Metabolic Disease. *Journal of Lipid Research* 2007; 48:1905-1914.

Guijarro, A., et al. Hypothalamic Integration of Immune Function and Metabolism. *Progress in Brain Research* 2006; 153:367-405.

Gunstad, J., et al. Relationship between Body Mass Index and Brain Volume in Healthy Adults. *International Journal of Neuroscience* 2008; 118(11):1582-1593.

Gustafson, D. R., et al. Adiposity Indicators and Dementia over 32 Years in Sweden. *Neurology* 2009; 73:1559-1566.

Gustafson, Deborah, et al. An 18-Year Follow-up of Overweight and Risk of Alzheimer Disease. *Archives of Internal Medicine* 2003; 163(13):1524-1528.

Heber, David. An Integrative View of Obesity. *American Journal of Clinical Nutrition* 2010; 91:280S-283S.

Higami, Y., et al. Energy Restriction Lowers the Expression of Genes Linked to Inflammation, the Cytoskeleton, the Extracellular Matrix, and Angiogenesis in Mouse Adipose Tissue. *Journal of Nutrition* 2006; 136:343-352.

Hunt, Katherine J., et al. Inflammation in Aging Part 1: Physiology and Immunological Mechanisms. *Biological Research in Nursing* 2010; 11:245-252.

Hunt, Katherine J., et al. Inflammation in Aging Part 2: Implications for the Health of Older People and Recommendations for Nursing Practice. *Biological Research in Nursing* 2010; 11:253-260.

Kahn, Steven E., et al. Obesity Is a Major Determinant of the Association of C-Reactive Protein Levels and the Metabolic Syndrome in Type 2 Diabetes. *Diabetes* 2006; 55:2357-2364.

Kang, Jae Hee, et al. Low Dose Aspirin and Cognitive Function in the Women's Health Study Cognitive Cohort. *British Medical Journal* 2007; 334:987-990.

Kern, Philip A., et al. Adiponectin Expression from Human Adipose Tissue: Relation to Obesity, Insulin Resistance, and Tumor Necrosis Factor-a Expression. *Diabetes* 2003; 52:1779-1785.

Knopman, David S., et al. Cardiovascular Risk Factors and Cerebral Atrophy in a Middle-aged Cohort. *Neurology* 2005; 65:876-881.

Komulainen, Pirjo, et al. Serum High Sensitivity C-Reactive Protein and Cognitive Function in Elderly Women. *Age and Ageing* 2007; 36(4):443-448.

Key References (cont'd)

Law, I. K., et al. Identifcation and Characterization of Proteins Interacting with SIRT1 and SIRT3: Implications in the Anti-aging and Metabolic Effects of Sirtuins. *Proteomics* 2009; 9(9):2444-2456.

Lee, Eon Sook, et. al. Depressive Mood and Abdominal Fat Distribution in Overweight Premenopausal Women. *Obesity Research* 2005; 13:320-325.

Lin, Ying, et al. The Hyperglycemia-induced Inflammatory Response in Adipocytes: The Role of Reactive Oxygen Species. *Journal of Biological Chemistry* 2005; 280(6): 4617-4626.

Logroscino, Giancarlo, et al. Prospective Study of Type 2 Diabetes and Cognitive Decline in Women Aged 70-81 Years. *British Medical Journal* 2004; 328:348.

Longo, V. D. Linking Sirtuins, IGF-I Signaling, and Starvation. *Experimental Gerontology* 2009; 44(1-2):70-74.

Lopez-Lluch, G., et al. Calorie Restriction Induces Mitochondrial Biogenesis and Bioenergetic Efficiency. *Proceedings of the National Academy of Sciences* 2006; 103:1766-1773.

Luchsinger, J.A., et al. Body Mass Index, Dementia, and Mortality in the Elderly. *Journal of Nutrition, Health & Aging* 2008; 12(2):127-31.

Luchsinger, Jose A., and Deborah R. Gustafson. Adiposity and Alzheimer's Disease. *Current Opinion in Clinical Nutrition and Metabolic Care* 2009; 12(1):15-21.

Luchsinger, Jose A., et al. Relation of Diabetes to Mild Cognitive Impairment. *Archives of Neurology* 2007; 64:570-575.

Ma, Qiu-Lan, et al. Omega-3 Fatty Acid Docosahexaenoic Acid Increases SorLA/LR11, a Sorting Protein with Reduced Expression in Sporadic Alzheimer's Disease (AD): Relevance to AD Prevention. *Journal of Neuroscience* 2007; 27(52):14299-14307.

Malin, Lonn, et al. Adipocyte Size Predicts Incidence of Type-2 Diabetes in Women. *FASEB Journal* 2010; 24:326-331.

Mamalakis, George, et al. Depression and Adipose Polyunsaturated Fatty Acids in an Adolescent Group. *Prostaglandins, Leukotrienes and Essential Fatty Acids* 2004; 71:289-294.

Mangge, H., et al. Low Grade Inflammation in Juvenile Obesity and Type 1 Diabetes Associated with Early Signs of Atherosclerosis. *Experimental and Clinical Endocrinology Diabetes* 2004; 112:378-382.

Martin, Bronwen, et al. Sex-dependent Metabolic, Neuroendocrine, and Cognitive Responses to Dietary Energy Restriction and Excess. *Endocrinology* 2007; 148:4318-4333.

McTiernan, Anne, et al. Exercise Effect on Weight and Body Fat in Men and Women. *Obesity* 2007; 15:1496-1512.

Nathan, C. Epidemic Inflammation: Pondering Obesity. *Molecular Medicine* 2008; 14(7-8):485-492.

Navarrete-Reyes, A. P., and M. Montana-Alvarez. Inflammaging. *Review of Investigational Clinics* 2009; 61(4):327-336.

Neels, Jaap G., and Jerrold M. Olefsky. Inflamed Fat: What Starts the Fire? *Journal of Clinical Investigation* 2006; 116:33-35.

Ng, Te-Pin, et al. Albumin, Haemoglobin, BMI and Cognitive Performance in Older Adults. *Age and Ageing* 2008; 37:423-429.

Nigro, Julie, et al. Insulin Resistance and Atherosclerosis. *Endocrine Reviews* 2006; 27(3):242-259.

Porte, Daniel, Jr., et al. Insulin Signaling in the Central Nervous System: A Critical Role in Metabolic Homeostasis and Disease from C. Elegans to Humans. *Diabetes* 2005; 54:1264-1276.

Pou, Karla M., et al. Visceral and Subcutaneous Adipose Tissue Volumes Are Cross-sectionally Related to Markers of Inflammation and Oxidative Stress. *The Framingham Heart Study. Circulation* 2007; 116:1234-1241.

Key References (cont'd)

Ravaglia, Giovanni, et al. Serum C-Reactive Protein and Cognitive Function in Healthy Elderly Italian Community Dwellers. *The Journals of Gerontology Series A: Biological Sciences and Medical Sciences* 2005; 60:1017-1021.

Rudin, Eric, and Nir Barzilai. Inflammatory Peptides Derived from Adipose Tissue. *Immunity & Ageing* 2005; 2:1.

Sammel, Mary D., et al. Weight Gain among Women in the Late Reproductive Years. *Family Practice* 2003; 20(4):401-409.

Sauve, A. A. Pharmaceutical Strategies for Activating Sirtuins. *Current Pharmacological Descriptions* 2009; 15(1): 45-56.

Savage, David B., et al. Disordered Lipid Metabolism and the Pathogenesis of Insulin Resistance. *Physiological Reviews* 2007; 87:507-520.

Schmidt, R., et al. Early Inflammation and Dementia: A 25-Year Follow-up of the Honolulu-Asia Aging Study. *Annals of Neurology* 2002; 52(2):168-174.

Seliger, Stephen L., et al. Moderate Renal Impairment and Risk of Dementia among Older Adults: The Cardiovascular Health Cognition Study. *Journal of the American Society of Nephrology* 2004; 15:1904-1911.

Shoba B., et al. Function of Sirtuins in Biological Tissues. *Anatomical Record* (Hoboken) 2009; 292(4):536-543.

Shoelson, S. E., et al. Obesity, Inflammation and Insulin Resistance. *Gastroenterology* 2007; 132(6):2169-2180.

Simon, Gregory, et al. Association between Obesity and Psychiatric Disorders in the U.S. Adult Population. *Archives of General Psychiatry* 2006; 63:824-830.

Speakman, J.R., and C. Hambly. Starving for Life: What Animal Studies Can and Cannot Tell Us about the Use of Caloric Restriction to Prolong Human Lifespan. *Journal of Nutrition* 2007; 137:1078-1086.

Steptoe, Andrew, et al. Neuroendocrine and Inflammatory Factors Associated with Positive Affect in Healthy Men and Women: The Whitehall II Study. *American Journal of Epidemiology* 2008; 167:96-102.

Storz, Peter. Reactive Oxygen Species---Mediated Mitochondria-to-Nucleus Signaling: A Key to Aging and Radical-caused Diseases. *Frontiers in Bioscience* 2005; 10:1881-1890.

Stote, K.S., et al. A Controlled Trial of Reduced Meal Frequency without Caloric Restriction in Healthy, Normal-weight, Middle-aged Adults. *American Journal of Clinical Nutrition* 2007; 85:981-988.

Suganami, Takayoshi, et al. Role of the Toll-like Receptor 4/NF-kB Pathway in Saturated Fatty Acid---Induced Inflammatory Changes in the Interaction between Adipocytes and Macrophages. *Arteriosclerosis, Thrombosis, and Vascular Biology* 2007; 27:84-91.

Szekely, C.A., et al. Nonsteroidal Anti-inflammatory Drugs for the Prevention of Alzheimer's Disease: A Systematic Review. *Neuroepidemiology* 2004; 23(4):159-169.

Tahara, E.B., et al. Dihydrolipoyl Dehydrogenase as a Source of Reactive Oxygen Species Inhibited by Caloric Restriction and Involved in Saccharomyces Cerevisiae Aging. *FASEB Journal* 2007; 21:274-283.

Taki, Y., et al. Relationship between Body Mass Index and Gray Matter Volume in 1,428 Healthy Individuals. *Obesity* (Silver Spring) 2008; 16(1):119-124.

Tedgui, Alain, and Ziad Mallat. Cytokines in Atherosclerosis: Pathogenic and Regulatory Pathways. *Physiological Reviews* 2006; 86:515-581.

Teli, Thalia, et al. Regulation of Appetite and Insulin Signaling in Inflammatory States. *Annals of the New York Academy of Sciences* 2006; 1083:319-328.

Trayhurn, P. Endocrine and Signalling Role of Adipose Tissue: New Perspectives on Fat. *ACTA Physiologica Scandinavica* 2005; 184:285-293.

Tsiotra, Panayoula C., and Constantine Tsigos. Stress, the Endoplasmic Reticulum, and Insulin Resistance. *Annals of the New York Academy of Sciences* 2006; 1083:63-76.

van den Berg, E., et al. The Impact of Diabetes Mellitus on Cognitive Decline in the Oldest of the Old: A Prospective Population-based Study. *Diabetologia* 2006; 49(9):2015-2023.

Key References (cont'd)

Varady, K.A., and M.K. Hellerstein. Alternate-day Fasting and Chronic Disease Prevention: A Review of Human and Animal Trials. *American Journal of Clinical Nutrition* 2007; 86:7-13.

Volkow, N. D., et. al. Inverse Association between BMI and Prefrontal Metabolic Activity in Healthy Adults. *Obesity* 2009; 17(1):60-65.

Ward, Michael A., et al. The Effect of Body Mass Index on Global Brain Volume in Middle-aged Adults: A Cross Sectional Study. *BMC Neurology* 2005; 5:23.

Watch Your Weight, Preserve Your Memory. *Mind, Mood & Memory*, April 2007. Massachusetts General Hospital.

Weisberg, Stuart P., et al. Obesity Is Associated with Macrophage Accumulation in Adipose Tissue. *Journal of Clinical Investigation* 2003; 112:1796-1808.

Wellen, Kathryn E., and Gokhan S. Hotamisligil. Inflammation, Stress, and Diabetes. *Journal of Clinical Investigation* 2005; 115(5):1111-1119.

West, Nancy A., and Mary N. Haan. Body Adiposity in Late Life and Risk of Dementia or Cognitive Impairment in a Longitudinal Community-based Study. *Journals of Gerontology Series A: Biological Sciences and Medical Sciences* 2009; 64A:103-109.

Whitmer, R.A., et al. Central Obesity and Increased Risk of Dementia More than Three Decades Later. *Neurology* 2008; 71:1057-1064.

Whitmer, Rachel A., et al. Obesity in Middle Age and Future Risk of Dementia: A 27 Year Longitudinal Population Based Study. *British Medical Journal* 2005; 330(7504):1360.

Witte, A.V., et al. Caloric Restriction Improves Memory in Elderly Humans. *Proceedings of the National Academy of Sciences* 2009; 106:1255-1260.

Xu, Haiyan, et al. Chronic Inflammation in Fat Plays a Crucial Role in the Development of Obesity-related Insulin Resistance. *Journal of Clinical Investigation* 2003; 112:1821-1830.

Young, Sara E., et al. Hyperinsulinemia and Cognitive Decline in a Middle-aged Cohort. *Diabetes Care* 2006; 29:2688-2693.

Following Chapter Five, "Resources" lists current books
that may be referenced in this chapter.

THE BRAIN

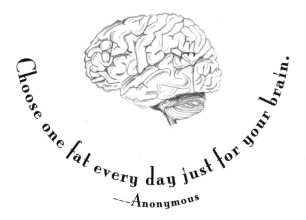

Choose one fat every day just for your brain.

---Anonymous

Chapter Three
Protection: Fat and the Brain

The Blood-Brain Barrier 82
   Crossing the barrier 82
   Piercing the barrier 86

The Fatty Brain 88
   Selecting healthful fats 88
   Controlling the flame 90

Omega-3s 95
   Resolvins/protectins: better than good 96
   Fish, oil, seeds 98
   The antidepressant: EPA or DHA? 102

 Conclusion 105

Brain Homework: Nutrition for a Hungry Brain
   Get Picky about Protein 105

Key References 107

"Barrier" is quite possibly
a poor description
of the blood-brain barrier.

---Laura Pawlak

The Blood-Brain Barrier

The brain is small but mighty. Weighing less than five percent of body weight, it utilizes about twenty percent of the available oxygen. Nutrients and oxygen are delivered by four arteries and their branches, forming an arterial circuit around the brain.

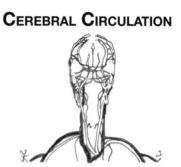

CEREBRAL CIRCULATION

Crossing the barrier

More than one hundred years ago, it was noted that a blue dye, injected into the bloodstream of an animal, would turn all tissues blue except the brain and spinal cord. The molecular structure of the blue dye was just too big to enter the brain. Scientists observed that blood vessels serving the central nervous system differ from the vessels around other organs. As blood travels from large arteries to the smallest vessels, called *capillaries*, the flow slows for efficient transfer of nutrients and oxygen into tissues. The large cross-sectional area of the capillaries provides adequate space for exchange between the blood and cells. To facilitate the process, blood capillaries have a wall only one cell-layer thick, consisting of a simple tissue called *endothelium*.

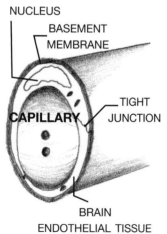

NUCLEUS
BASEMENT
MEMBRANE
CAPILLARY
TIGHT JUNCTION
BRAIN
ENDOTHELIAL TISSUE

Careful investigation of the capillaries around the brain reveals unique features. The naturally occurring openings (pores) in the capillary wall are absent. Tight, continuous junctions between the endothelial cells give the appearance of a barrier between the body and the brain. These anomalies create a cellular barrier between the blood and neurons---the *blood-brain barrier*.

The barrier is the gatekeeper, screening all chemicals attempting to enter the brain. Neurochemicals, such as serotonin, norepinephrine, dopamine, and gamma-aminobutyric acid, are barred from the brain, as neurons synthesize them in response to internal and external stimuli.

An exception: Very limited amounts of the excitatory neurotransmitters *glutamate* and *aspartate* in the blood cross into the brain. Thus, the consumption of glutamate as monosodium glutamate (MSG) and aspartate in the artificial sweetener aspartame remain unproved yet possible, subtle stimulants of emotional and behavioral abnormalities.

What's the Point?
In treating Parkinson's disease, the precursor for dopamine, L-dopa, must be administered. L-dopa crosses the barrier, but dopamine cannot reach the brain. Enzymes stand ready in the barrier to destroy dopamine or any chemical that resembles the shape of dopamine.

ENDOTHELIAL BARRIER

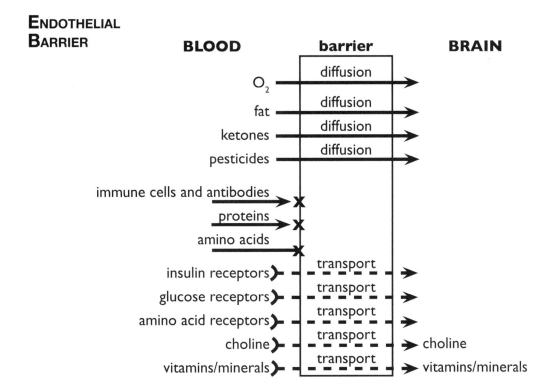

Some molecules simply walk through the barrier, a process called *diffusion*. For example, water and gases, such as oxygen and carbon dioxide, enter freely.

As like attracts like, the fatty barrier is fat-friendly. Fatty acids from the diet move rapidly through it. Pesticides and many other man-made toxic chemicals are lipid-soluble and, unfortunately, pass freely into the brain, contributing to neurodegeneration.

Water-soluble molecules, such as proteins, amino acids, glucose, and other substances with an electrical charge are slow to pass through the barrier, if they do at all. Instead, transporters specific for each substance carry these molecules into the brain.

For example, choline is the precursor for the neurochemical acetylcholine, essential for memory functions and learning. A choline-specific carrier at the barrier limits the amount of choline entering the brain regardless of the amount of choline you swallow in food or in a pill. Too much choline is not good for the brain, but enough is important. Chapter Five lists food sources of choline.

Your diet and supplements supply the brain with vitamins and minerals. The transport system for various vitamins and minerals has a low capacity since the brain recycles all these vital nutrients. The brain utilizes vitamins and minerals at a rapid pace yet cannot synthesize nor store them. Reliance on dietary intake could be fatal, especially in times of famine. Recycling vitamins and minerals is a smart solution. Examples of vitamin/mineral deficiencies and their effects on the central nervous system are discussed on the next page.

ABOUT VITAMIN AND MINERAL DEFICIENCIES IN THE BRAIN

DEFICIENCY	EFFECTS ON THE CENTRAL NERVOUS SYSTEM
Thiamin, B-1	loss of myelin sheath, headache
Niacin, B-3	confusion, disorientation, depression, memory deficit, mania, paranoia
Pyridoxine, B-6	mania, convulsions, poor production of GABA, serotonin, dopamine
Folate	memory disorder, convulsions
Cobalamin, B-12	memory, pain, degeneration of white matter
Vitamin D	seizures, restlessness (calcium deficit), inflammatory neurodegeneration
Vitamin C	oxidation, neurodegeneration
Vitamin E	oxidation, neurodegeneration
Iron	altered cognition
Magnesium	anxiety, headache, insomnia
Zinc	hallucinations, depression, fetal brain defects
Boron	mood disorders
Source: faculty.washington.edu/chudler/nutr2html	

Folate, a dynamite vitamin! It works against cancers, heart attacks, strokes, high blood pressure, hearing loss, and depression---all affecting cognition. High blood levels of folate are linked to faster thought processing and enhanced memory, if vitamin B-12 status is normal.

Microorganisms in the soil produce B-12. In the good old days, eating a little soil on freshly picked garden vegetables was not considered problematic. Today, plant foods are ultraclean when purchased---no soil.

Vitamin K has a new focus. The vitamin lowers the blood levels of fourteen inflammatory cytokines. You'll find the best food choices of vitamin K, and all the vitamins and minerals, in Chapter Five, "Nutrition and the Prevention of Alzheimer's."

Piercing the barrier

The blood-brain barrier plays a critical role in the connection between the central nervous system and peripheral tissues. The unique position of the barrier, with one side facing the blood and the other facing the brain, means that substances can be secreted from the barrier into the body, into the brain, or both.

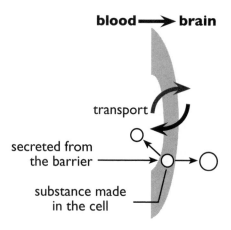

blood ⟶ brain

transport

secreted from the barrier ⟶

substance made in the cell

BRAIN ENDOTHELIAL CELL

William Banks finds that secretions from the barrier not only influence peripheral and central nervous system events but can act to coordinate them. It's all so perfect, unless chemical events cause weakening, denaturation, and penetration of the barrier.

Decay of the barrier means increased permeability of potentially harmful substances into the brain. Many factors can disrupt the barrier, such as infection, emotional stress, hypertension, ischemia, oxidation, nicotine, insomnia, air pollution, pesticides and other chemicals that cause oxidation, the many chronic inflammatory diseases, and untreated mood disorders.

What's the Point?

Breaking down the barrier is a goal, not a problem, when you are trying to deliver therapeutic drugs to brain tumors. Neurosurgeons at Cedars-Sinai Hospital discovered a naturally occurring peptide, bradykinin, that temporarily opens the barrier, allowing drug delivery to a brain tumor. The procedure causes no harm to healthy brain tissue and, although still experimental, has great promise.

Lupus erythematosus is an autoimmune disease inducing chronic inflammation, potentially throughout the body. If the disease-related inflammation also creates a breach in the blood-brain barrier, antibodies gain access to the brain. These antibodies cause atrophy of hippocampal neurons, resulting in the cognitive dysfunction observed in some lupus patients.

In the case of multiple sclerosis, the individual is genetically vulnerable to lifestyle factors that pierce the blood-brain barrier. T-cells from the peripheral immune system penetrate the barrier and inflame the myelin sheath. Neurodegeneration ensues. How do you protect your barrier? The kinds of fats you eat will strengthen or weaken the blood-brain barrier.

LOOK ALIKE, ACT ALIKE

Nothing crosses a solid barrier. Fats, called *saturated* and *trans*, are solid at room temperature. Saturates and trans fats look alike and produce similar structures and functions in the body and brain. The harder the fat---such as lard---the more saturates and/or trans fatty acids in the food.

COOH COOH

111°

123°

Saturated Fat

Trans Fat

The blood-brain barrier must be semi-permeable, requiring fluidity. The small amount of solid fat required for stabilization of the barrier and all cell membranes can be manufactured by the liver. In contrast, essential fats---the dietary fats that cannot be synthesized in the body---are obtained from fish and plant foods. Choose liquid or soft fats and let your liver add the solids needed to complete the blood-brain barrier. The next section, "The Fatty Brain," describes the structural and functional properties of dietary fats and their position in the fight against dementia.

The Fatty Brain

If your lifestyle mirrored your Stone Age ancestors', there would be no need to balance fats in your diet. In those times, humans consumed what was provided from the earth, with little alteration. If you could return to that era, your diet would naturally provide the right balance of fats for your brain. Going back to that primitive lifestyle is unthinkable. What is reasonable in a world with so many processed foods? Sift through the marketing nonsense and find the right combination of fats to protect your hungry brain. Welcome to the challenge!

Selecting healthful fats

Excluding adipose tissue, the nervous system has the greatest concentration of fat-like substances called *lipids*. The brain is primarily a fat-based organ, with almost sixty percent of the tissue composed of lipids. Lipids are the core materials for the membranes of cells in the blood-brain barrier, for neuron membranes, and for the fatty sheaths surrounding the axons of neurons. That's a lot of lipid!

A diet with a balance of the essential fatty acids---omega-6s and omega-3s---works effectively with the immune system to initiate and terminate inflammatory responses. The diet of long ago probably achieved near equal amounts of essential fatty acids. Animals roamed and obtained omega-3s from the grasses. Feeding on sea vegetables, fish consumed and stored a significant amount of omega-3s. The plentiful supply of seeds and nuts provided ample amounts of omega-6s.

Animal fat is highly saturated and practically devoid of omega-3s, unless animals are left to graze in grassy fields. As pristine lakes and oceans vanish, fish may ingest and store mercury and other chemicals---not a comforting thought.

THE BUIILDING BLOCKS OF LIPIDS

Kind of Fat	Form	Notes
Saturated Fatty Acids	solid	Not required, made by liver, excess unhealthy Sources: meat and dairy fat, palm and coconut oils
Trans Fatty Acids	solid	Act as saturates, unhealthful, artificial, little in nature Sources: hydrogenated fats
Unsaturated Fats		Natural, healthful, balance is important
Omega-9s	liquid	Monounsaturates, not essential, from diet or made in body Sources: olives, almonds, avocado
Omega-6s	liquid	Polyunsaturates, essential, from diet only Sources: plant oils Arachidonic acid is converted primarily to inflammatory hormones. The exception is gamma-linolenic acid, suppressing inflammation. **Arachidonic Acid** (omega-6)
Omega-3s	liquid	Polyunsaturates, essential, from diet only Sources: fish, flax, walnuts Eicosapentaenoic acid, EPA, is converted to anti-inflammatory hormones. Docosahexaenoic acid, DHA, has non-hormonal anti-inflammatory actions and other supportive activities for brain and barrier. **Docosahexaenoic acid** (omega-3)

Fats are now processed, rather than eaten in their natural form. Oil is pressed from the corn, soybeans, and various nuts and seeds, intensifying the intake of omega-6s from plants. Meanwhile, the consumption of saturated and trans fatty acids soars.

Critter Diary

It was summer. Angel was two years old. I was chatting with the horse shoer when I noticed Angel wheezing. Summer in Arizona brings a swarm of allergens, and she certainly was a victim---allergic asthma. I was told that Angel's life span would be significantly diminished as the inflammation destroyed her lungs like a wildfire in the forest.

Since adding ground flax seeds, turmeric, and fish oil to her food, Angel's breathing has become deeper and less labored. All of these natural products dampen the inflammatory response in her lungs. With poor oxygen capacity, Angel was lethargic and gaining weight, contributing to the severity of her disease. Along with her weight loss, I kept her active, as muscle releases anti-inflammatory cytokines into the circulation during exercise. At times, she runs and hoots as she did in the good old days before asthma. Lifestyle makes a difference.

Controlling the flame

At the core of an inflammatory response are lipids essential for life---the omega-3 and omega-6 families of fatty acids. With only minor differences in shape, these two families share the same enzymes, yet their end products have significantly different effects on brain function and structure.

The building materials for the members of these two families are molecules eighteen carbons long, obtained from plants. The many double bonds in these liquid fats begin either on the third or sixth carbon, accounting for their family names, *omega-3* and *omega-6*.

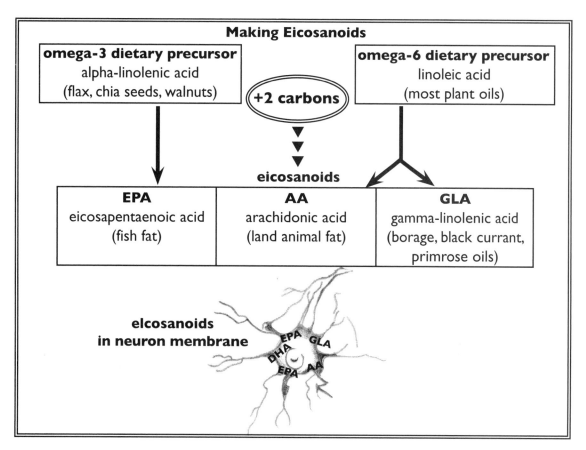

With the addition of two carbons, the twenty-carbon fatty acids formatted from omega-3 and omega-6 plant precursors are called *eicosanoids*. Eicosanoids can also be obtained directly: eicosapentaenoic acid (EPA) from fish; arachidonic acid (AA) from land animal fat; gamma-linolenic acid (GLA) from borage, primrose, and black currant oils. Regardless of the source, eicosanoids are stored in membranes of all brain and body cells.

Similar to the National Guard, ready to jump into uniform and repel any local intruders, eicosanoids are quickly converted into hormones that attack a local injury or insult. Just add oxygen and the proper enzymes to the three eicosanoids (EPA, AA, GLA) and an array of hormonal compounds are formed, with specific functions related to local inflammation.

Localized Inflammatory Hormones from EPA, AA, GLA		
Prostaglandins pain, inflammation	**Thromboxanes** clotting, vasoconstriction	**Leukotrienes** allergies, autoimmune disease

These short-acting hormones, released from glial cells and neurons, are effective in exceedingly low concentrations.

Prostaglandins are the major inflammatory responders in the brain. The intensity of an inflammatory response is related to the various fats in your diet. As the brain ages, uncontrolled expression of these short-acting hormones contributes to the neuroinflammation observed in Alzheimer's and other neurodegenerative diseases.

Prostaglandin Production eicosanoids		
EPA eicosapentaenoic acid (fish fat, algae)	**AA** arachidonic acid (land animal fat)	**GLA** gamma-linolenic acid (borage, black currant, primrose oils)
▼▼▼	▼▼▼	▼▼▼
Prostaglandin E3 **reduces** inflammatory response	Prostaglandin E2 inflammatory response	Prostaglandin E1 **reduces** inflammatory response

Note: Naming prostaglandin groups as strong or weak inflammatory agents is a generalization, with individual exceptions, such as lipoxins, highly anti-inflammatory prostaglandins derived from arachidonic acid in the presence of low-dose aspirin. The thromboxane and leukotriene products of eicosanoids are not shown here.

In spite of the omega-6 surname, gamma-linolenic acid and its end products are stirring up interest. In addition to the unique prostaglandins made from gamma-linolenic acid, this fatty acid acts directly against inflammation by suppressing T-cells, the immune cells initiating an inflammatory response. Patients with inflammatory disorders show more improvement when combining gamma-linolenic acid with omega-3 fatty acids than with omega-3s alone. Maximizing any and all mechanisms that dampen inflammation in the brain means including gamma-linolenic acid in your lifestyle.

Lacking food sources, supplements of borage oil (20-26% GLA), black currant seed oil (14-19% GLA), or primrose oil (7-10% GLA) are available. Be mindful that your diet can interfere with the effectiveness of gamma-linolenic acid in your body and your brain. An excess of alcohol, dietary cholesterol, trans fatty acids, saturated fats, or sugar (as in high-fructose corn syrup) can slow production of this healthful prostaglandin.

What about the foods containing about seventy percent of their oil as monounsaturated fatty acids: olives/oil, avocados/oil, macadamia nuts/oil, almonds/oil, hazelnuts/oil, and pecans? Research supports monounsaturated fatty acids---often called omega-9s as their first and only double bond is on the ninth carbon---against all aging diseases. The structure of omega-9s is stable, naturally deterring decay and inflammation. Monounsaturated oils are great substitutes for an excess intake of omega-6s, prominent in corn oil, sunflower oil, and safflower oil.

The Bottom Line!
In place of the slogan "Where's the meat?"
how about, "Where are the 3s, 6s, and 9s?"

MORE
About essential fatty acid imbalances

The combined consumption of omega-6 unsaturated fatty acids, trans fatty acids, and saturated fatty acids has dramatically increased the ratio of pro-inflammatory to anti-inflammatory lipids in the American diet. If the intake of omega-3s is insufficient, omega-6s are substituted, but there may be clinical consequences:

First, a decrease of omega-3s in neuron membranes alters enzyme activity by twenty to forty percent, even if the total unsaturated fatty acid content in the membrane is identical.

Second, during fetal development, a low maternal intake of omega-3s is correlated with fewer vesicles in the hippocampus for the storage of neurotransmitters. After birth, as fewer neurotransmitters per unit of time are available, memory processing is slower. Impaired learning in children or cognitive decline in mid-age adults is noticeable, as illustrated here.

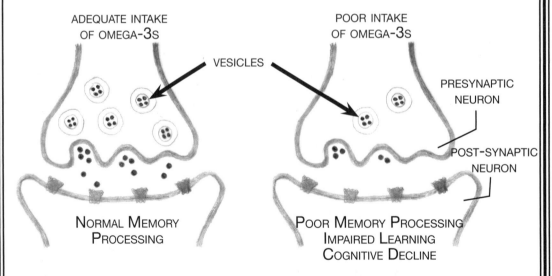

ADEQUATE INTAKE
OF OMEGA-3S

POOR INTAKE
OF OMEGA-3S

VESICLES

PRESYNAPTIC
NEURON

POST-SYNAPTIC
NEURON

NORMAL MEMORY
PROCESSING

POOR MEMORY PROCESSING
IMPAIRED LEARNING
COGNITIVE DECLINE

Third, as junk food is added to a diet deficient in omega-3s, the higher ratio of saturated fat (solid fat) alters the fluidity of neuron membranes, affecting memory and learning. Fluidity allows the flow of information---an impulse---as ions travel in and out of the membrane. Chapter Four has the details and drawings.

Fourth, the brain is more sensitive to the mineral lead when the percentage of omega-3s is low, as omega-3s confer resistance to neurotoxicity.

Can you become what you eat? Yes. Mice fed fish oil for twelve months showed more brain omega-3s and less brain omega-6s, more synaptic membrane fluidity, and higher maze-learning ability. That's encouraging!

The Bottom Line!
Diet makes a difference. Feel the difference for yourself.

Omega-3s

Beyond the hormones generated by EPA, researchers can't contain their curiosity about the benefits of DHA in the brain.

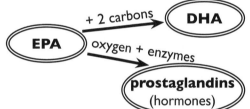

The two fatty acids of importance in the omega-3 family, eicosapentaenoic acid (EPA) and docosahexaenoic acid (DHA), are required nutrients for the brain. EPA and DHA differ in both size and function. Overall, human tissue contains five- to thirty-fold more DHA than EPA. In the brain and retina, however, DHA is several hundred-fold more abundant than EPA.

The high content of DHA is reflected in rapid communication among neurons and the generation of new neurons, especially in the hippocampus, where learning begins. DHA is important in the protection against brain diseases, such as Alzheimer's and Parkinson's diseases. Led by William S. Harris and coworkers, studies are underway to follow cognitive decline in persons taking various doses of purified DHA.

Of all the fatty acids, omega-3s are the major biological regulators of the immune response. Best known for their hormonal work as prostaglandins, suppressing inflammation, omega-3s also act through nonhormonal mechanisms to temper the immune response. The nonhormonal derivatives of omega-3s reduce the number of inflammatory cytokines released from the brain's and body's immune cells. Trials using fish oil for the treatment of chronic inflammatory diseases report fewer inflammatory cytokines in persons treated with fish oil than in those with placebos. Good news!

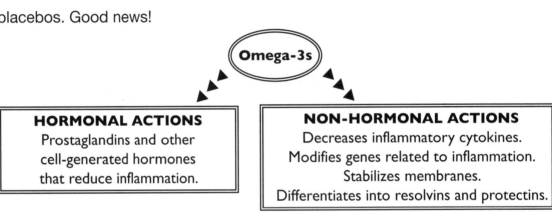

Resolvins/protectins: better than good

Since 2006, interest in EPA and DHA has been drifting toward the study of their derivatives, *resolvins* and *protectins*. The term "resolvins" or resolution-phase interaction products was coined by Charles Serhan and colleagues. Resolvins attenuate inflammation and resolve ongoing inflammatory injury. Protectins act more like shields against neurodegeneration.

Resolvins and protectins are about one thousand times more potent than the parent molecules, EPA and DHA. The derivatives of EPA were named resolvins of the E series. Both resolvins and protectins derived from DHA were labeled as the D series. Isolation of the various resolvins and protectins is underway and several clinical applications are currently in clinical trials.

Resolvins and protectins have a number of well-documented healthful effects in the brain: inhibitory effects on inflammatory hormones produced by the neuron; suppression of inflammatory cytokines, T-cells, and other inflammatory immune cells; the formation of a diverse number of novel biologically active mediators of inflammation; positive effects on insulin sensitivity; and resolution of inflammation in the retina and brain cells. These derivatives are extremely protective for the cardiovascular system, a plus for the brain.

Surprise! Resolvins are also derived from omega-6 fatty acids. In 2009, Bindi Dangi and coworkers reported that both gamma-linolenic acid (GLA) and docosapenaenoic acid (DPA), omega-6 fatty acids, can resolve inflammation. Although arachidonic acid is the precursor of inflammatory prostaglandins, interest in the resolvins derived from omega-6s, not just omega-3s, is ignited. Presently clinical practitioners prioritize omega-3s as the major agents against inflammation.

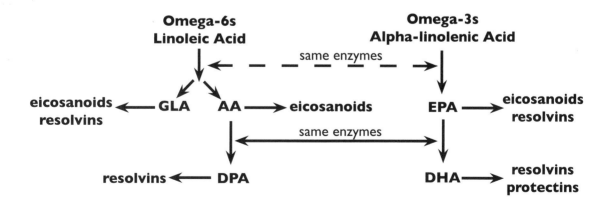

MORE
About medications against inflammation

Potent immunosuppressive agents, like cyclosporin, decrease inflammation at the price of suppressing your entire immune system. Corticosteroids decrease chronic inflammatory diseases by blocking the production of arachidonic acid, and thus all protaglandins, good and bad, are reduced. Over-the-counter therapies, such as aspirin and NSAIDS, work by blocking inflammation and pain but also block the mucosal protection in the gastrointestinal tract. All of these products have potential side effects, such as gastrointestinal bleeding.

With a natural program, you eat more foods with omega-3 fatty acids. The enzymes that synthesize prostaglandins simply interact with more omega-3s than omega-6s.

Metabolic pathways are not disturbed. Other healthful functions of

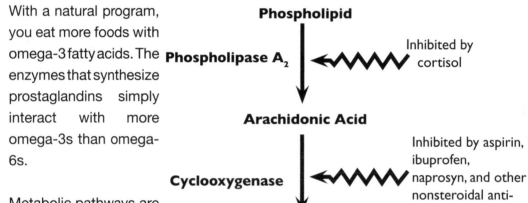

these fatty acids are unaltered, such as their effects on blood levels of triglycerides and high-density lipoproteins (HDLs), blood pressure, growth, vision, learning, and tissue repair.

Fish, oil, seeds

It is always best to get EPA and DHA from food. For example, fish contains a variety of nutrients that complement the activity of omega-3s, such as selenium and protein.

Fish oil is a natural anticoagulant. Contrary to previous thinking, however, concerns about excessive bleeding from the intake of omega-3 capsules seems unfounded. According to University of California scientists, 2009, interaction with anti-clotting medication or aspirin is theoretically possible, but no risk has been noted with doses as high as four grams per day. However, six grams or more per day may increase blood sugar in type-2 diabetics. Additionally, analyses of fish oil capsules did not find significant levels of mercury or other contaminants, whether inexpensive or pricey.

DHA is the important fatty acid for cognition and vision in persons of all ages, but the greatest dependency on dietary DHA occurs during the development of the central nervous system. Lactating women who eat fish or consume fish oil capsules express DHA in breast milk. Hormone-induced changes in gene expression during pregnancy and lactation were assumed to enhance maternal DHA production from flax, the plant precursor of DHA, to meet the needs of the fetus and newborn. Cindy Francois' research did not support this hypothesis. Pregnant and lactating women taking flaxseed did not show a significant increase of DHA in their milk.

S. D. Doughman and coworkers reported that adults convert only ten to fifteen percent of ingested alpha-linolenic acid in flax or other plants to EPA. Ideally, only five percent of EPA could be expected as DHA in the brain. Rather than rely on fetal conversion of EPA to DHA, it was recommended that pregnant women consume fish or fish oil capsules to assure optimum DHA.

Chia seeds have the highest percentage of omega-3s in the plant world. You don't have to grind the seeds to maximize the absorption of the oil, as recommended with flax seeds. A. G. Chicco studied dietary chia seeds in rats fed a sucrose-rich diet, which stimulates inflammation. Whole chia seeds, ground seeds, or chia oil improved insulin sensitivity and decreased LDL values and visceral fat triggered by the sucrose-rich diet. Compliance issues were minimal. Still, the seed is more difficult to find, more pricey than flax seed, and has not been tested for percent conversion to DHA.

The research of Linda Arterburn and coworkers brought more clarity regarding the value of plant-based omega-3s. Conversion of alpha-linolenic to EPA and DHA varies with metabolic need and dietary intake of omega-3s versus omega-6s. Researcher Gwendolyn Barcelo- Coblijn added more support to the belief in plant sources of omega-3s. In her study, adults consumed either flax oil, fish oil, or sunflower oil (high in omega-6s) for three months. The omega-3 content of human red blood cells was found to be dose-dependent. Consuming 2.5 to 3.5 grams of flax oil per day elevated red-blood-cell EPA and DHA and lowered inflammatory markers equivalent to a fish oil intake of 0.5 to 1.0 gram per day.

Generally, the conversion of plant precursors to EPA and DHA may maintain normal health, but doubt remains that protective tissue levels of EPA and DHA are possible with the exclusive intake of plant food sources, according to William Harris and coworkers. Harris concludes that the plant format is not a surrogate omega-3. Worth noting as an exception are microalgae and seaweeds, sources of EPA and/or DHA. In clinical trials, algae is comparable to fish oil in lowering plasma triglycerides and inflammation.

Several organic, refined algal oils are available with 100 to 200 mg of DHA per pill. However, most foods with added DHA from algae contain only 32 mg in a serving.

Biochemists and geneticists are contemplating alternative solutions for vegans desiring more EPA and DHA from plant-based foods. Development of gene-modified flax seeds can increase the content of *stearidonic acid*, an omega-3 fatty acid that bypasses the limiting step in the synthesis of EPA. A genetically altered soybean oil with stearidonic acid is also being developed. More EPA means more DHA---assuming the public accepts gene-modified foods.

OMEGA-3 FATTY ACID CONTENT OF SELECTED FOODS

Source	Portion	Total omega-3
Animal	**(as EPA and DHA)**	**Fatty acids (grams)**
Salmon, canned, drained	4 ounces	2.2
Mackerel, canned, drained	4 ounces	2.2
Salmon, cold water, fresh and frozen, cooked	4 ounces	1.7
Sardines, canned in oil, drained	4 ounces	1.8
Tuna, canned in water, drained	4 ounces	0.3
Plant	**(as ALA)**	
Walnuts	1 ounce	2.6
walnut oil	1 Tablespoon	1.4
Flax seeds	1 ounce	1.8
flax oil	1 Tablespoon	6.9
canola oil	1 Tablespoon	1.3

Source: Tufts School of Medicine: med-nutrition-infection@tufts.edu

Note: When comparing the omega-3 content of animal foods to plant foods, a calculation is required. Multiply the grams of omega-3s in the plant food by 10%. Use this adjusted number to compare the plant's omega-3 content to an equal quantity of an animal source . Only about one-tenth of the alpha-linolenic acid in the plant source is synthesized into EPA within the body.

MORE
About fish oil capsules

The brain contains lipids highly enriched with phosphorus. Does the claim that fish is good brain food refer to the phosphorus-containing lipids in both fish and human brains? Nachum Vaisman and associates, 2008, reported that children with attention deficit disorder responded better to fish fats carried as phospholipids rather than as triglycerides, the standard format in capsules. His claim remains a theory until further research brings clarity to the dispute.

The oil from krill can also be encapsulated. This small crustacean congregates in dense masses, adding a red/pink color to the ocean surface. Krill contain smaller amounts of omega-3s per gram than standard cold-water fish but more antioxidants, noted by their color. *Astaxanthin* in krill is the main carotene pigment in these aquatic animals.

Although astaxanthin is a good source of carotenes, the concentration of the antioxidant per capsule and its effectiveness is unknown. This carotene accumulates naturally in wild salmon as they eat krill and other sea creatures that feed on astaxanthin-rich algae. Astaxanthin is added to fish feed consumed by farmed salmon. Without it, the salmon would have gray-colored flesh.

The antidepressant: EPA or DHA?

Recent studies point to a deficit of omega-3s as associated with depression. For example, societies that consume only a small amount of omega-3 fatty acids appear to have a higher prevalence of major depressive disorder. Still, clinical trials evaluating the antidepressant effect of omega-3s have mixed results. Most of the research has examined fish intake or fish oil capsules. The structural and functional differences between EPA and DHA have led investigators to purify these fatty acids and evaluate their relative effects on depression.

Is DHA an antidepressant? The concentration of DHA in neuron membranes is several hundredfold higher than that of EPA. DHA deficiency is associated with a decreased number of receptors for serotonin, norepinephrine, and dopamine. These neurochemicals affect mood. Magnetic resonance imaging (MRI) of the brain also reveals that the more DHA consumed, the more neurons in the hippocampus. Remodeling of the hippocampus, with a significant loss of neurons, is observed in brain scans of persons with prolonged, untreated depression. Is DHA then the key omega-3 fatty acid related to the etiology of mood dysfunction and the cognitive changes associated with depression?

On the other hand, EPA is an eicosanoid, readily converted into prostaglandins. These hormones are extremely potent in tiny amounts regulating inflammation that could cause structural remodeling of the hippocampus---causal for depression. EPA plays an important role in resolving fatigue, restoring normal sleep, and sharpening cognitive memory---all symptoms of depression. Is EPA the choice to combat depression?

Those who favor EPA must weigh their preference against the potential of this purified fish oil product to impair glucose tolerance. Elevated fasting glucose was reported in type-2 diabetics consuming large doses of purified EPA, but not DHA. A limited dose of EPA (less than 1.8 grams per day) can resolve this side effect.

What's the Point?
The cannabinoids inhaled from smoking marijuana or consumed in marijuana brownies interfere with the anti-inflammatory effects of omega-3 fatty acids. Additionally, persons with a high production of endocannabinoids, as noted in obesity, experience fewer benefits of a diet enriched with omega-3s.

Promoting one purified fatty acid over the other remains a subject for debate and should be evaluated on an individual basis. Omega-3s in fish or fish oil offer support solely for mild or moderate mood disturbances and seem most helpful as an adjunct to medication. The subtle differences in mood with pure EPA or DHA may be difficult to distinguish.

Notable for the elderly population, the synthesis of EPA and DHA from plant precursors slows with age by as much as 50 percent. A direct source of EPA and DHA is preferred for seniors, most importantly if a mood disorder has been diagnosed. Catherine Feart and her French coworkers found a clear relationship between high-plasma levels of EPA and milder symptoms in 1,400 elderly subjects treated for clinical depression. The significance was greater when antidepressants were combined with omega-3s.

More manufacturers are offering fish oil capsules containing various ratios of EPA to DHA as well as purified EPA and DHA products. These are unproved therapeutic approaches for mood disorders. Consult your medical professional before consuming purified EPA or DHA as a therapeutic agent.

In the future, resolvins and protectins may be more effective for the brain than either EPA or DHA. Overall, the need for more omega-3s cannot be ignored---regardless of the format.

> **The Bottom Line!**
> *Omega-3 fatty acids in food*
> *are essential to protect your hungry brain.*

Conclusion

Knowing your blood-brain barrier and fatty brain are vulnerable to inflammation, defense is simple. Eat liquid fat. Consciously choose and use more foods high in monounsaturates---olives, avocados, almonds, hazelnuts, pecans, and macadamia nuts. Fish first, when it comes to animal protein.

Nutritional interventions for treating
chronic neurodegenerative diseases,
such as Alzheimer's Disease,
will be focused on reducing or terminating
the chronic inflammatory response.

---Mark DeLegg

Brain Homework: Nutrition for a Hungry Brain
Get Picky about Protein

The brain homework helps you to continue to Think Body Fat and Think Inflammation. The protein you eat may come with lots of baggage in the form of saturated fat. Cut calories and inflammation by choosing proteins with less saturated fat.

The following foods are listed by protein content, from highest to lowest. For simplicity, the portion of the food is five ounces. The saturated fat in the five-ounce portion is averaged as high, medium, or low.

Food 5 ounce portion	Protein approx. grams	Saturated Fat Rating
lamb	50	high
beef sirloin	50	high
duck	40	high
pork	40	medium
chicken	40	medium
turkey	40	low
fish, high fat	40	low
fish, low fat	40	low
cheese (pizza)	35	very high
egg white only	35	trace
crab	30	trace
lobster	30	trace
soybeans	25	low
black-eyed peas	20	trace
whole egg	18	medium
peanut butter cookies	14	high
kidney beans	10	trace
salami	7	medium
garbanzo beans	7	trace
chocolate cake/frosting	7	high
seeds, nuts (1oz. only)	6	low
spinach	6	trace
broccoli	5	trace
ice cream	5	high
milk, 2%	5	low
California avocado	3	low
yellow corn	3	trace
banana	trace	trace
apple	trace	trace

For the saturated fat and other nutrient values of various foods: www.fnic.nal.usda.gov/

Key References

Aeberli, Isabelle, et al. Dietary Intakes of Fat and Antioxidant Vitamins Are Predictors of Subclinical Inflammation in Overweight Swiss Children. *American Journal of Clinical Nutrition* 2006; 84(4):748-755.

Andersen, L.P., et al. Gastric Inflammatory Markers and Interleukins in Patients with Functional Dyspepsia Treated with Astaxanthin. *FEMS Immunology and Medical Microbiology* 2007; 50(2):244-248.

Arterburn, Linda M., et al. Distribution, Interconversion, and Dose Response of N-3 Fatty Acids in Humans. *American Journal of Clinical Nutrition* 2006; 83(suppl):1467S-1476S.

Austria, J. Alejandro, et al. Bioavailability of Alpha-linolenic Acid in Subjects after Ingestion of Three Different Forms of Flaxseed. *Journal of the American College of Nutrition* 2008; 27:214-221.

Ayerza, R. Jr., and W. Coates. Effect of Dietary Alpha-linolenic Fatty Acid Derived from Chia when Fed as Ground Seed, Whole Seed and Oil on Lipid Content and Fatty Acid Composition of Rat Plasma. *Annals of Nutrition and Metabolism* 2007; 51(1):27-34.

Banks, William A. Blood-brain Barrier and Energy Balance. *Obesity* 2006; 14:234S-237S.

_____. Denial versus Dualism: The Blood-brain Barrier as an Interface of the Gut-brain Axis. *Endocrinology* 2006; 147(6):2609-2610.

Barcelo-Coblijn, Gwendolyn, et al. Flaxseed Oil and Fish-oil Capsule Consumption Alters Human Red Blood Cell n-3 Fatty Acid Composition: A Multiple-dosing Trial Comparing 2 Sources of n-3 Fatty Acid. *American Journal of Clinical Nutrition* 2008; 88:801-809.

Batetta, Barbara, et al. Endocannabinoids May Mediate the Ability of (n-3) Fatty Acids to Reduce Ectopic Fat and Inflammatory Mediators in Obese Zucker Rats. *Nutrient Physiology, Metabolism, and Nutrient-nutrient Interactions* 2009; 139:1495-1501.

Brooks, Tracy A., et al. Chronic Inflammatory Pain Leads to Increased Blood-brain Barrier Permeability and Tight Junction Protein Alterations. *American Journal of Physiology - Heart and Circulatory Physiology* 2005; 289:H738-H743.

Caider, P.C. Polyunsaturated Fatty Acids and Inflammatory Processes: New Twists in an Old Tale. *Biochimie* 2009; 91(6):791-795.

Chicco, A.G., et al. Dietary Chia Seed (Salvia hispanica L.) Rich in Alpha-linolenic Acid Improves Adiposity and Normalises Hypertriacylglycerolaemia and Insulin Resistance in Dyslipaemic Rats. *British Journal of Nutrition* 2009; 101(1):41-50.

Chilton, Floyd H., et al. Mechanisms by Which Botanical Lipids Affect Inflammatory Disorders. *American Journal of Clinical Nutrition* 2008; 87(2):498S-503S.

Curtis, Luke. Comment on: Guidelines for the Management of Hospital-acquired Pneumonia in the UK: Report of the Working Party on Hospital-acquired Pneumonia of the British Society for Antimicrobial Chemotherapy. *Journal of Antimicrobial Chemotherapy* 2008; 62:641.

Dangi, Bindi, et al. Biogenic Synthesis, Purification, and Chemical Characterization of Anti-inflammatory Resolvins Derived from Docosapentaenoic Acid (DPAn-6). *Journal of Biological Chemistry* 2009; 284:14744-14759.

Dartt, D.A., et al. Pro-inflammatory Leukotriene LTD4-stimulated Conjunctival Goblet Cell Secretion Is Blocked by the Resolvins RvE1 and RvD1. *Investigative Ophthalmology & Visual Science* 2009; 50:E-Abstract 4622.

Das, Undurti N. Essential Fatty Acids and Their Metabolites Could Function as Endogenous HMG-CoA Reductase and ACE Enzyme Inhibitors, Anti-arrhythmic, Anti-hypertensive, Anti-atherosclerotic, Anti-inflammatory, Cytoprotective, and Cardioprotective Molecules. *Lipids in Health and Disease* 2008; 7:37.

Deckelbaum, Richard J., et al. Omega-3 Fatty Acids and Gene Expression. *American Journal of Clinical Nutrition* 2006; 83(6):1520S-1525S.

de Groot, Renate H.M., et al. Effect of Alpha-linolenic Acid Supplementation during Pregnancy on Maternal and Neonatal Polyunsaturated Fatty Acid Status and Pregnancy Outcome. *American Journal of Clinical Nutrition* 2004; 79(2):251-260.

DeMar, James C., Jr., et al. Effect of Dietary Docosahexaenoic Acid on Biosynthesis of Docosahexaenoic Acid from Alpha-linolenic Acid in Young Rats. *Journal of Lipid Research* 2008; 49:1963-1980.

Deutsch, Luisa. Evaluation of the Effect of Neptune Krill Oil on Chronic Inflammation and Arthritic Symptoms. *Journal of the American College of Nutrition* 2007; 26(1):39-48.

Key References (cont'd)

Doughman, S.D., et al. Omega-3 Fatty Acids for Nutrition and Medicine: Considering Microalgae Oil as a Vegetarian Source of OPA and DHA. *Current Diabetes Reviews* 2007; 3(3):198-203.

Egert, Sarah, et. al. Dietary Alpha-linolenic Acid, EPA, and DHA Have Differential Effects on LDL Fatty Acid Composition but Similar Effects on Serum Lipid Profiles in Normolipidemic Humans. *Journal of Nutrition* 2009; 139:861-868.

Feart, Catherine, et al. Plasma Eicosapentaenoic Acid Is Inversely Associated with Severity of Depressive Symptomatology in the Elderly: Data from the Bordeaux Sample of the Three-city Study. *American Journal of Clinical Nutrition* 2008; 87(5):1156-1162.

Fernandez-Real, Jose-Manuel, et al. Insulin Resistance, Inflammation, and Serum Fatty Acid Composition. *Diabetes Care* 2003; 26:1362-1368.

Francois, Cindy A., et al. Supplementing Lactating Women with Flaxseed Oil Does Not Increase Docosahexaenoic Acid in Their Milk. *American Journal of Clinical Nutrition* 2003; 77(1):226-233.

Furse, Robert K., et al. Gammalinolenic Acid, an Unsaturated Fatty Acid with Anti-inflammatory Properties, Blocks Amplification of IL-1B Production by Human Monocytes. *Journal of Immunology* 2001; 167:490-496.

Gao, Fei, et al. Whole-body Synthesis-secretion Rates of Long-chain n-3 PUFAs from Circulating Unesterified Alpha-linolenic Acid in Unanesthetized Rats. *Journal of Lipid Research* 2009; 50:749-758.

Gonzalez-Periz, Ana, et al. Obesity-induced Insulin Resistance and Hepatic Steatosis Are Alleviated by w-3 Fatty Acids: A Role for Resolvins and Protectins. *FASEB Journal* 2009; 23(6):1946-1957.

Gottrand, Frederic. Long-chain Polyunsaturated Fatty Acids Influence the Immune System of Infants. *Journal of Nutrition* 2008; 138:1807S-1812S.

Guillemin, Gillies J., and Bruce J. Brew. Microglia, Macrophages, Perivascular Macrophages, and Pericytes: A Review of Function and Identification. *Journal of Leukocyte Biology* 2004; 75:388-397.

Haibin, Tian, et. al. Resolvins E1 and D1 in Choroid-Retinal Endothelial Cells and Leukocytes: Biosynthesis and Mechanisms of Anti-Inflammatory Actions. *Investigations in Ophthalmology and Visual Science* 2009; 50:3613-3620.

Halldorsson, Th.I., et al. Is High Consumption of Fatty Fish during Pregnancy a Risk Factor for Fetal Growth Retardation? A Study of 44,824 Danish Pregnant Women. *American Journal of Epidemiology* 2007; 166:687-696.

Harris, William S., et al. Towards Establishing Dietary Reference Intakes for Eicosapentaenoic and Docosahexaenoic Acids. *Journal of Nutrition* 2009; 139:804S-819S.

Hassan, Iram R., and Karsten Gronert. Acute Changes in Dietary w-3 and w-6 Polyunsaturated Fatty Acids Have a Pronounced Impact on Survival following Ischemic Renal Injury and Formation of Renoprotective Docosahexaenoic Acid-derived Protectin D1. *Journal of Immunology* 2009; 182:3223-3232.

Hawkins, Brian T., et al. Modulation of Cerebral Microvascular Permeability by Endothelial Nicotinic Acetylcholine Receptors. *American Journal of Physiology - Heart and Circulatory Physiology* 2005; 289:H212-H219.

He, Chengwei, et. al., Improved Spacial Learning Performance of Fat-1 Mice Is Associated with Enhanced Neurogenesis and Neuritogenesis by Docosaexaenoic Acid. *Proceedings of the National Academy of Sciences* 2009; 106:11370-11375.

Ikeuchi, M., et al. Effects of Astaxanthin in Obese Mice Fed a High-fat Diet. *Bioscience, Biotechnology, and Biochemistry* 2007; 71(4):893-9.

Innis, Sheila M., and Russell W. Friesen. Essential n-3 Fatty Acids in Pregnant Women and Early Visual Acuity Maturation in Term Infants. *American Journal of Clinical Nutrition* 2008; 87:548-557.

Jin, Yiping, et al. Novel Anti-inflammatory and Pro-resolving Lipid Mediators Block Inflammatory Angiogenesis. *Investigative Ophthalmology & Visual Science*, April 2009;10.1167/lovs.08-2462.

Karppi, J., et al. Effects of Astaxanthin Supplementation on Lipid Peroxidation. *International Journal for Vitamin and Nutrition Research* 2007; 77(1):3-11.

Kasuga, Kie, et al. Rapid Appearance of Resolvin Precursors in Inflammatory Exudates: Novel Mechanisms in Resolution. *Journal of Immunology* 2008; 181:8677-8687.

Kaul, Nalini, et al. A Comparison of Fish Oil, Flaxseed Oil and Hempseed Oil Supplementation on Selected Parameters of Cardiovascular Health in Healthy Volunteers. *Journal of the American College of Nutrition* 2008; 27:51-58.

Key References (cont'd)

Kiecolt-Glaser, Janice K., et al. Depressive Symptoms, Omega-6:Omega-3 Fatty Acids, and Inflammation in Older Adults. *Psychosomatic Medicine* 2007; 69:217-224.

Kowal, Czeslawa, et al. Human Lupus Autoantibodies against NMDA Receptors Mediate Cognitive Impairment. *Proceedings of the National Academy of Sciences* 2006; 103(52):19854-19859.

Leedom, A.J., et al. Increased Ratio of Dietary w-3 Pufa Induces Formation of DHA-derived Lipid Autacoids That Inhibit Inflammatory Neovascularization in the Cornea. *Investigative Ophthalmology & Visual Science* 2009; 50:4956.

Lien, Vanessa W., and Michael T. Clandinin. Dietary Assessment of Arachidonic Acid and Docosahexaenoic Acid Intake in 4-7 Year-old Children. *Journal of the American College of Nutrition* 2009; 28:7-15.

Lucas, Michel, et al. Ethyl-eicosapentaenoic Acid for the Treatment of Psychological Distress and Depressive Symptoms in Middle-aged Women: A Double-blind, Placebo-controlled, Randomized Clinical Trial. *American Journal of Clinical Nutrition* 2009; 89:641-651.

Madden, Sarah M.M., et al. Direct Diet Quantification Indicates Low Intakes of (n-3) Fatty Acids in Children 4 to 8 Years Old. *Journal of Nutrition* 2009; 139:528-532.

Mayer, K., and W. Seeger. Fish Oil in Critical Illness. *Current Opinion in Clinical Nutrition and Metabolic Care* 2008; 11(2):121-127.

McNamara, R.K., et al. Deficits in Docosahexaenoic Acid and Associated Elevations in the Metabolism of Arachidonic Acid and Saturated Fatty Acids in the Postmortem Orbitofrontal Cortex of Patients with Bipolar Disorder. *Psychiatry Research* 2008; 160(3):285-299.

Miranda, B., et al. Self-perceived Memory Impairment and Cognitive Performance in an Elderly Independent Population with Age-related White Matter Changes. *Journal of Neurology, Neurosurgery & Psychiatry* 2008; 79:869-873.

Mori, Trevor A., et al. Purified Eicosapentaenoic and Docosahexaenoic Acids Have Differential Effects on Serum Lipids and Lipoproteins, LDL Particle Size, Glucose, and Insulin in Mildly Hyperlipidemic Men. *American Journal of Clinical Nutrition* 2000; 71(5):1085-1094.

Niu, Shui-Lin, et al. Reduced G Protein-coupled Signaling Efficiency in Retinal Rod Outer Segments in Response to n-3 Fatty Acid Deficiency. *Journal of Biological Chemistry* 2004; 279(30):31098-31104.

Okuyama, Hidtoshi, et. al., Significance of Antioxidative Functions of Eicosapentaenoic and Docosahexaenoic Acids in Marine Microorganisms. *Applied and Environmental Microbiology* 2008; 74(3):570-574.

Parihar, Mordhwaj S., and Gregory J. Brewer. Mitoenergetic Failure in Alzheimer Disease. *American Journal of Physiology - Cell Physiology* 2007; 292:C8-C23.

Parker, Gordon, et al. Omega-3 Fatty Acids and Mood Disorders. *American Journal of Psychiatry* 2006; 163:969-978.

Pontes-Arruda, Alessandro, et al. The Use of an Inflammation-modulating Diet in Patients with Acute Lung Injury or Acute Respiratory Distress Syndrome: A Meta-analysis of Outcome Data. *Journal of Parenteral and Enteral Nutrition* 2008; 32:596-605.

Rapoport, Stanley I. Arachidonic Acid and the Brain. *Journal of Nutrition* 2008; 138:2515-2520.

Riediger, N.D., et al. Low n-6:n-3 Fatty Acid Ratio, with Fish- or Flaxseed Oil, in a High Fat Diet Improves Plasma Lipids and Beneficially Alters Tissue Fatty Acid Composition in Mice. *European Journal of Nutrition* 2008; 47(3):153-160.

Reinoso, M.A., et al. Expressions Are Down-regulated by Resolvins in Retinal Pigment-epithelial (arpe-19) Cells. http://highwire.stanford.edu/cgi/gca?allch (accessed 2/1/09).

Resolvins and Protectins. The Lipid Library. http://www. lipidlibrary.co.ukl/Lipids (accessed 2/1/09).

Rogers, P.J., et al. No Effect of n-3 Long-chain Polyunsaturated Fatty Acid (EPA and DHA) Supplementation on Depressed Mood and Cognitive Function: A Randomised Controlled Trial. *British Journal of Nutrition* 2008; 99(2):421-31.

Samieri, Cecilia, et al. Low Plasma Eicosapentaenoic Acid and Depressive Symptomatology Are Independent Predictors of Dementia Risk. *American Journal of Clinical Nutrition* 2008; 88:714-721.

Sapieha, P., et al. Dietary Intake of w-3 Polyunsaturated Fatty Acids Promotes an Anti-angiogenic Lipidomic Profile in the Retina. *Investigative Ophthalmology & Visual Science* 2009; 50:4308.

Key References (cont'd)

Sarin, H., et. al., Metabolically Stable Bradykinin B2 Receptor Agonists Enhance Transvascular Drug Delivery into Malignant Brain Tumors by Increasing Drug Half-life. *Journal of Translational Medicine* 2009; 7:33.

Serhan, C.N. Controlling the Resolution of Acute Inflammation: A New Genus of Dual Anti-inflammatory and Proresolving Mediators. *Journal of Periodontology* 2008; 79(8 Suppl):1520-1526.

Serhan, C.N., et al. Resolving Inflammation: Dual Anti-inflammatory and Pro-resolution LIpid Mediators. *Nature Reviews Immunology* 2008; 8(5):349-361.

Serhan, Charles N., et al. Resolvins: A Family of Bioactive Products of Omega-3 Fatty Acid Transformation Circuits Initiated by Aspirin Treatments that Counter Proinflammation Signals. *Journal of Experimental Medicine* 2002; 196(8):1025-1037.

Shaikh, Saame Raza, and Michael Edidin. Polyunsaturated Fatty Acids, Membrane Organization, T Cells, and Antigen Presentation. *American Journal of Clinical Nutrition* 2006; 84(6):1277-1289.

Simopoulos, Artemis. Omega-3 Fatty Acids in Inflammation and Autoimmune Diseases. *Journal of the American College of Nutrition* 2002; 21(6):495-505.

Song, Cai, et al. Long-chain Polyunsaturated Fatty Acids Modulate Interleukin-1B-induced Changes in Behavior, Monoaminergic Neurotransmitters, and Brain Inflammation in Rats. *Journal of Nutrition* 2008; 138:954-963.

Streit, Wolfgang J., et al. Microglia and Neuroinflammation: A Pathological Perspective. *Journal of Neuroinflammation* 2004; 1:14.

Struzynska, Lidia, et al. Inflammation-like Glial Response in Lead-exposed Immature Rat Brain. *Toxicological Sciences* 2007; 95(1):156-162.

Su, K.P. Mind-body Interface: The Role of n-3 Fatty Acids in Psychoneuroimmunology, Somatic Presentation, and Medical Illness Comorbidity of Depression. *Asia Pacific Journal of Clinical Nutrition* 2008; 17(Suppl 1):151-157.

Tian, Haibin, et al. Resolvins E1 and D1 in Choroid-retinal Endothelial Cells and Leukocytes: Biosynthesis and Mechanisms of Anti-inflammatory Actions. *Investigative Ophthalmology & Visual Science*, May 2009;10.1167/iovs.08-3146.

Umezawa, Makiko, et al. Effect of Dietary Unsaturated Fatty Acids on Senile Amyloidosis in Senescence-accelerated Mice. *Journals of Gerontology Series A: Biological Sciences and Medical Sciences* 2009; 64A:646-652.

Vaisman, Nachum, et al. Correlation between Changes in Blood Fatty Acid Composition and Visual Sustained Attention Performance in Children with Inattention: Effect of Dietary n-3 Fatty Acids Containing Phospholipids. *American Journal of Clinical Nutrition* 2008; 87(5):1170-1180.

van de Rest, Ondine, et al. Effect of Fish-oil Supplementation on Mental Well-being in Older Subjects: A Randomized, Double-blind, Placebo-controlled Trial. *American Journal of Clinical Nutrition* 2008; 88(3):706-713.

Vedin, Inger, et al. Effects of Docosahexaenoic Acid-rich n-3 Fatty Acid Supplementation on Cytokine Release from Blood Mononuclear Leukocytes: The OmegAD Study. *American Journal of Clinical Nutrition* 2008; 87:1616-1622.

Waitzberg, Dan Linetzky, and Raquel Susana Torrinhas. Fish Oil Lipid Emulsions and Immune Response: What Clinicians Need to Know. *Nutrition in Clinical Practice* 2009; 24:487-499.

Weaver, Kelly L., et al. Effect of Dietary Fatty Acids on Inflammatory Gene Expression in Healthy Humans. *Journal of Biological Chemistry* 2009; 284:15400-15407.

Weitzel, L.R., et al. Effects of Pharmaconutrients on Cellular Dysfunction and the Microcirculation in Critical Illness. *Current Opinion in Anaesthesiology* 2009; 22(2):177-83.

Yu, Yongmei, et al. Reciprocal Interactions of Insulin and Insulin-like Growth Factor I in Receptor-mediated Transport across the Blood-brain Barrier. *Endocrinology* 2006; 147(6):2611-2615.

Zhang, F., et al. Resolvins Stimulate Human Corneal Epithelial Cell Migration. *Investigative Ophthalmology & Visual Science* 2008; 49:3396.

Zhang, X., et al. Impact of Astaxanthin-enriched Algal Powder of Haematococcus Pluvialis on Memory Improvement in BALB/c Mice. *Environmental Geochemistry and Health* 2007; 29(6):483-9.

Following Chapter Five, "Resources" lists current books
that may be referenced in this chapter.

THE BRAIN

Eating whole foods gratifies your brain.

---Anonymous

Chapter Four
Mysterious Links: Nutrients and Neurons

A Neuron at Work 114
   Glucose and the mighty mitochondria 114
   Electrolytes create action 117
   Chemicals of communication 119
   Proteins at the synapse 121

Preventing Neuron Decay 122
   Oxidative stress 123
   Antioxidants 126
   Enzymes 126
   Networks 126
   Stars 128
   Supplements 136

Nutrients, a Summary 140

 Conclusion 141

Brain Homework: Nutrition for a Hungry Brain
   Improve your redox number 141

Key References 143

By its work, we know the neuron.

---Laura Pawlak

A Neuron at Work

When referring to the brain, the old statement, "You are what you eat," is better stated as, "You become what you eat." Neurons respond to your diet. So say good-bye to fast food, prepackaged meals, or just plain junk. Upgrade the nutrient reservoir in your brain and you'll rejuvenate the working efficiency of neurons.

A Neuron at Work

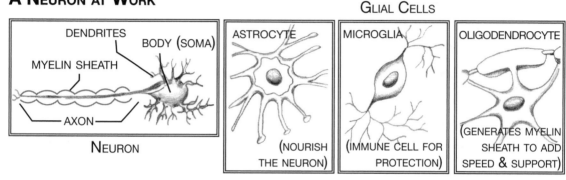

GLIAL CELLS

NEURON

ASTROCYTE (NOURISH THE NEURON)

MICROGLIA (IMMUNE CELL FOR PROTECTION)

OLIGODENDROCYTE (GENERATES MYELIN SHEATH TO ADD SPEED & SUPPORT)

Improving your intake of nutrient-rich food maintains glial cells in good working order as well. Glial cells support, protect, and nourish the neuron. They dispose of waste material. They accelerate the speed of an impulse by manufacturing an insulating sheath, called the *myelin sheath*, around axons. Glial cells are the unsung heroes of the brain.

No other cell in the human organism can compete with the work capacity of a neuron. Let's see how it all happens.

Glucose and the mighty mitochondria

Work requires energy. The source of energy for a neuron is glucose, not fat. Glucose is delivered to the brain without the aid of insulin. Special transporters whisk the fuel past the blood-brain barrier into neurons and their fuel-burning furnaces, mitochondria.

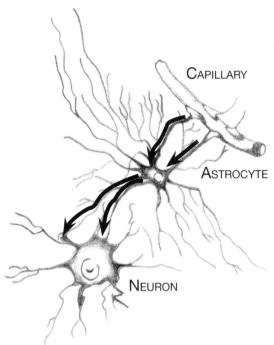

CAPILLARY

ASTROCYTE

NEURON

The transport of glucose from the barrier to each neuron is facilitated by astrocytes located between the blood vessel and the neurons. The end feet of astrocytes attach to the blood capillary. Glucose enters the astrocyte, is partially metabolized, and then deposited in the neuron.

With the help of oxygen, enzymes sever the chemical bonds holding the atoms of glucose in place. Although much of the energy obtained from glucose is lost as heat, a portion is captured in the bonding of phosphate molecules to an adenosine molecule. The brain is thus supplied with "gasoline" called *adenosine triphosphate* (ATP). On demand, the phosphate molecules are separated from the adenosine framework and the energy released is utilized for various metabolic needs within neurons and glial cells. The adenosine molecule is recycled into ATP as glucose is supplied by the diet. Persons consuming a low carbohydrate diet perform poorly in memory tests as compared to persons with an adequate intake of carbohydrate---a clean-burning, quick source of ATP.

Why not break down fat molecules from adipose tissue into ATP? Fat generates ATP too slowly to meet the metabolic needs of brain cells. The neuron is thus dependent on glucose for energy from your diet and small amounts released from the liver. When a neuron is deprived of sufficient glucose, hunger diverts your thoughts to foods high in sugar.

MORE
About the neuron's energy needs

Neuron metabolism is extremely sensitive to diet. A high carbohydrate diet (78%) that is low in protein (10%) markedly decreases brain glucose utilization and ATP supply. Even a marginal dietary deficiency of protein, when coupled with a carbohydrate-rich diet, reduces the amount of glucose metabolized in the neuron. The brain processes perceptions slowly and learning is affected. Children are especially vulnerable to eating a huge amount of sugar and white flour while protein-rich foods may be sparsely consumed.

Carbohydrates are a great source of energy when the source is natural food. Still, dietary protein is the building material for specific enzymes that convert glucose into energy (ATP). The silent cofactors of these enzymes are B-vitamins. Enzymes are nonfunctional without their cofactors. That's why neurons don't perform well on junk food. The junk food diet is often loaded with sugar and fat but low in protein and B-vitamins.

During fetal brain development and the first few years of life, protein malnutrition rapidly shrinks the body (soma) of the neuron, the length of dendrites, and the number of dendrite branches. Neurons in the hippocampus are the most seriously affected, accounting for the learning disabilities of malnourished children.

How much protein should you consume each day? The answer varies with age, gender, and special needs. The adult should aim for fifteen to thirty percent of the diet as lean protein. Consult a registered dietitian to calculate your protein requirements accurately.

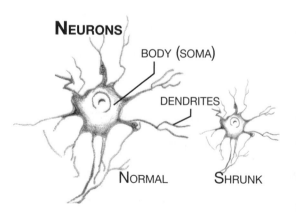

NEURONS

BODY (SOMA)

DENDRITES

NORMAL   SHRUNK

Why do children who skip breakfast do poorly in school? Glucose provides more than energy for learning. The acetyl portion of the neurochemical acetylcholine is a derivative of glucose.

Acetylcholine-producing neurons are numerous in the hippocampus, aiding memory processing, and in the areas of the brain that permanently store information. After a long night's fast, acetylcholine can be rapidly depleted as the brain is highly challenged in the classroom or workplace. Where's the glucose for brain fuel and acetylcholine? In your breakfast.

BREAKFAST + CONCENTRATION = ACETYLCHOLINE

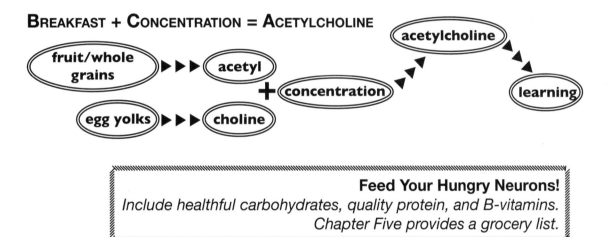

Feed Your Hungry Neurons!
Include healthful carbohydrates, quality protein, and B-vitamins.
Chapter Five provides a grocery list.

Electrolytes create action

All your sensations, movements, thoughts, and emotions are accomplished by the talk among neurons. This communication is executed by two interdependent processes: *Electrical conduction* and *chemical transmission*.

NEURONAL COMMUNICATION

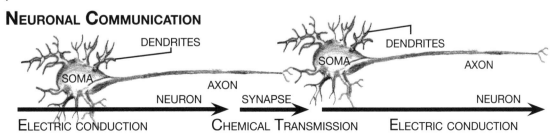

ELECTRICAL CONDUCTION

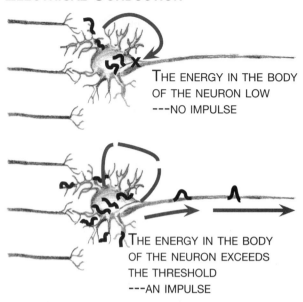

THE ENERGY IN THE BODY
OF THE NEURON LOW
---NO IMPULSE

THE ENERGY IN THE BODY
OF THE NEURON EXCEEDS
THE THRESHOLD
---AN IMPULSE

NEURON AT REST

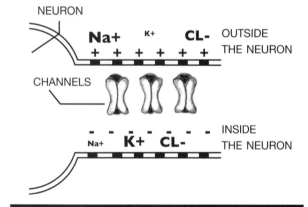

NEURON

Na+   K+   CL-   OUTSIDE
+ + + + + +   THE NEURON

CHANNELS

- - - - - -   INSIDE
Na+   K+   CL-   THE NEURON

NEURON IMPULSE TRAVELS

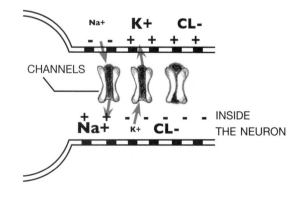

Na+   K+   CL-
- - + + + +

CHANNELS

+ + - - - - -   INSIDE
Na+   K+   CL-   THE NEURON

In electrical conduction, the zap of an impulse begins as neurochemicals fit into matching receptors on the dendrites of a neuron. Similar to electricity, the impulse travels down the dendrites to the cell body (soma). If the intensity of the impulse at the soma falls below the neuron's ignition threshold, communication terminates. If the intensity exceeds the threshold, then a nerve impulse travels down to the tip of the axon, causing neurochemicals in axon vesicles to eject into the synapse.

Impulses are generated by inorganic molecules, known as *electrolytes*, moving in and out of a neuron through proteins embedded in the membrane, called *channels*. The channels open and close, allowing the flow of electrolytes---sodium and potassium---to create an impulse. Dietary sources of sodium and potassium are critical for the flow of information from neuron to neuron.

The balance of sodium to potassium is as basic to brain activity as the alphabet is to language. Excessive sweating may threaten sodium balance if the replacement fluid is devoid of salt, but the major dietary deficit is sufficient potassium, abundant in fruits and vegetables. Electrolyte imbalance may present as high blood pressure, confusion, lethargy, or seizures.

> **Feed Your Working Neurons!**
> *Emphasize potassium-containing foods*
> *to balance electrical conduction through the neuron.*
> *Chapter Five lists the best.*

Chemicals of communication

> *You are your synapses.*
> *They are who you are.*
>
> ---Joseph LeDoux

Neurons communicate with one another without direct contact. Neuron A produces chemicals meant to reach neuron B. The transmission of chemicals from A to B occurs within a space, the synapse, bridging the gap between the two neurons. The synapse also offers the opportunity to spread chemicals to nearby neurons in other circuits, adding speed and diversity to brain functions.

The flow of energy through a neuron---the impulse---would serve no purpose if not to synthesize and release chemicals into the synapse. The neurochemicals reach receptors on the dendrites of adjacent neurons and the impulse continues forward as the chemicals slip into receptors.

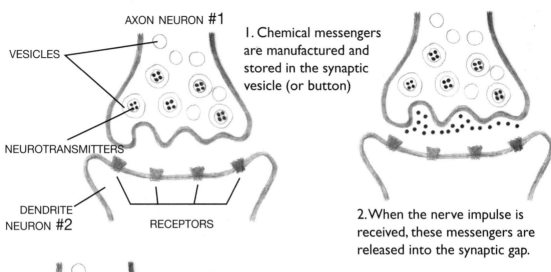

AXON NEURON #1

VESICLES

NEUROTRANSMITTERS

DENDRITE NEURON #2

RECEPTORS

1. Chemical messengers are manufactured and stored in the synaptic vesicle (or button)

2. When the nerve impulse is received, these messengers are released into the synaptic gap.

3. Like keys in a lock, these messengers are then recognized by receptors in the membrane of the next neuron. By activating these receptors, the messengers regenerate the nerve impulse in this neuron.

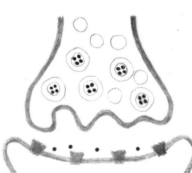

4. Lastly, the messengers must be quickly deactivated to free up the receptors and make them available for the next stimulus.

Visually the synapse appears as empty space, occupied only by fluid. Wisely, the brain leaves nothing to chance, and certainly not something as important as the chemical energy for working neurons. Astrocytes envelop synapses so intimately that they are thought to compartmentalize the spaces between neurons with the appearance of a spider's web.

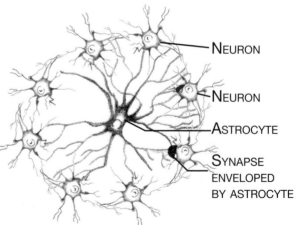

NEURON

NEURON

ASTROCYTE

SYNAPSE ENVELOPED BY ASTROCYTE

The astrocytes are silent players in the transmission of an impulse. The astrocytes increase the power of the brain to adapt, to learn, to remember. Here's how it works: The number of neurotransmitters released from the terminals of the presynaptic neuron is related to the concentration of calcium ions (an excitatory electrolyte) in the synapse. It is proposed that astrocytes control the amount of calcium available in the synapse.

PRESYNAPTIC NEURON

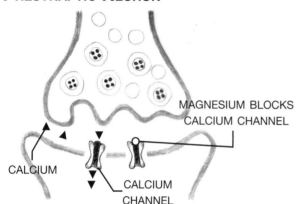

MAGNESIUM BLOCKS
CALCIUM CHANNEL

CALCIUM

CALCIUM
CHANNEL

Equally important is magnesium. This ion blocks entry of calcium into neurons until the appropriate moment, preventing hyperexcitability and possible damage to the brain by excess calcium.

> **Feed Your Working Neurons!**
> *Beyond bone, the balance of magnesium to calcium controls chemical conduction at the synapse. Find great food sources for these ions in Chapter Five.*

Proteins at the synapse

In contrast to carbohydrates and fats, proteins are nitrogen-containing molecules. The small units of a protein, amino acids, are the building blocks of excitatory neurotransmitters, such as glutamate, and quieting transmitters, as in gamma-aminobutyric acid, GABA.

PROTEIN UTILIZATION
IN WORKING NEURONS

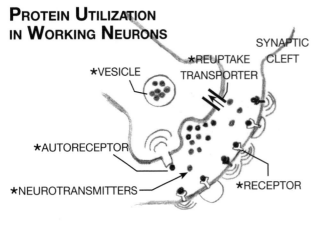

*proteins, peptides, or amino acids

Humans produce a repertoire of about 30,000 different proteins that act as operators of cellular functions and structural elements in the brain. Every protein has its own sequence, shape, and purpose. The three-dimensional format of a protein creates a pocket that is the active site of enzymes or the conformation of structures within the neuron.

When exposed to oxidation and inflammation, proteins misfold. Misfolding destroys the function of the protein and its solubility in the fluid medium, water. The clumps of protein, unless removed, interfere with the conduction of impulses and are associated with neurodegeneration and disease, such as Alzheimer's.

> **Feed your working neurons!**
> *Protein is essential*
> *for neuron communication.*
> *Read about the best sources in Chapter Five.*

Preventing Neuron Decay

Inflammation is the evil twin of oxidation.
Where you find one, you find the other.

---James Joseph

The synergy of oxidation and inflammation is a fundamental obstacle in the pursuit of an efficient brain. Oxidation initiates decay and inflammation enhances the process. Antioxidants can thus play a pivotal role in resisting the first step in the death of a neuron---oxidation.

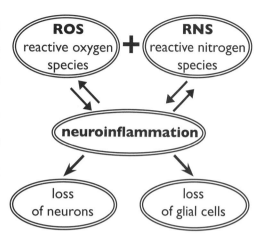

Oxidative stress

Oil gets rancid, and fruit turns brown. All organisms living in an aerobic environment are continually exposed to the chemical products of oxidation. *Reactive oxygen species* are the causal molecules of oxidation.

Reactive oxygen and nitrogen metabolites were identified decades ago and termed *free radicals*. Whether the species is called free or reactive, these molecules are unstable. When more reactive species are generated than are neutralized, the chemical environment within and around neurons is labeled as *oxidative stress*. The result is decay---unless antioxidants neutralize the reactive species.

Reactive species are by-products of normal aerobic metabolism. Of all the structures in a neuron, the mitochondria have the highest concentrations of oxygen and produce the greatest number of reactive species. Oxidative decay of the mitochondria is disastrous. Because this structure generates fuel, mitochondrial depletion creates an energy-poor environment that hastens the demise of the working neuron. Uncontrolled, reactive species also cause widespread instability of all fatty structures---not good news for the fatty brain and blood-brain barrier.

MITOCHONDRIA
(HIGHLY VULNERABLE
TO OXIDATIVE STRESS)

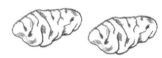

Antioxidants also act against inflammation. The formation of pro-inflammatory prostaglandins from omega-6 fatty acids is inhibited by antioxidants, as illustrated in the diagram.

ANTIOXIDANTS TARGET INFLAMMATION

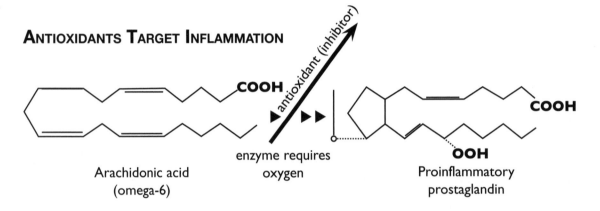

Arachidonic acid (omega-6) — enzyme requires oxygen — Proinflammatory prostaglandin

Still, oxidation is not totally bad news. As oxidative stress spirals upward in mitochondria, the oxidized chemicals signal genes that rally the production of antioxidants and anti-inflammatory cytokines. It's the 911 call to your mitochondrial DNA. This mechanism is observed during endurance training.

Avid runners have a greater exposure to oxygen during exercise and their neurons need more protection against oxidation than do those of the typical active person. In a study of oxidative stress, researchers gave a high dose of antioxidant supplements to endurance athletes and none to athletes in the control group.

After four weeks, only the athletes not taking the supplements improved the number of antioxidant enzymes in brain and body cells. Supplements suppressed the cells' natural protective mechanisms against reactive species. There's a lesson here! Lifestyle makes a difference in the oxidative environment within neurons.

Factors that generate reactive species include physical, mental, and emotional stressors, exposure to radiation, pathological conditions, pathogens, chemicals such as pesticides or herbicides, UV light, smoking, pollution in the air or water, infection, inflammatory diseases, and mood disorders. The battle against oxidative stress is ongoing. The threat to brain health is escalating.

What about your diet? The more calories you consume the more oxidative stress generated in mitochondria, especially if the foods consumed are fatty, processed, or loaded with preservatives.

Critter Diary

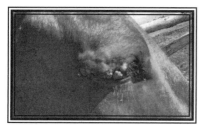

When I adopted three-year-old Noah, he had approximately twenty tumors (sarcomas) around his right upper eyelid. Three surgeries later, the tumors continued to appear. Would removal of the eye be the next step?

I tried an alternative approach, ozone injected directly into his vein followed by oral ozone salt. The tumors receded and disappeared. Cancer cells have a high rate of metabolism. Did the ozone preferentially trigger a damaging blow by escalating the production of reactive oxygen species to the cancer cells? Was it just coincidence, good luck? Perhaps future research will reveal the answer. Meanwhile, Noah enjoys his new status---in remission.

> **Shield Your Working Neurons!**
> *Uncontrolled oxidation causes inflammation.*
> *Your grocery list in Chapter Five has antioxidant-dense foods.*

Antioxidants

An antioxidant is a bodyguard. When oxidants approach, the antioxidant has two strategies: First, act: neutralize reactive species. Second, get help: activate the expression of genes that convert omega-3 fatty acids into anti-inflammatory prostaglandins and other protective factors, such as resolvins and protectins, discussed in Chapter Three. The teamwork of omega-3 fatty acids and antioxidants is essential for preserving neurons.

Enzymes

A number of sophisticated antioxidant enzymes patrol the neuron in search of reactive species. These enzymes are inactive without their mineral cofactors. You make the difference between a working and resting enzyme by supplying these minerals from your diet. For example, the most potent antioxidant enzyme, *superoxide dismutase*, needs zinc, copper, and manganese, while other antioxidant enzymes require iron or selenium.

Feed your antioxidant enzymes their required cofactors!
Zinc, copper, manganese, iron,
and selenium are present in food.
See your grocery list, Chapter Five.

Networks

Aid your biodefense. Eat plant foods to increase your antioxidant power. Vitamin C works in water-soluble areas. The entire fat-soluble family of vitamin E protects membranes within the blood-brain barrier, as well as neuron and glial membranes. It was earlier assumed that vitamins C and E worked independently. Instead, it is now known that a number of antioxidants act in concert with vitamins C and E, forming an antioxidant network in the brain.

The network recycles antioxidants from the oxidized state (inactive) to the reduced state (active), retaining a high *redox number*---the ratio of active to inactive antioxidants. Still, a diet loaded with fruits and vegetables makes the network hum with available antioxidants and provides a constant supply of minerals for antioxidant enzymes.

The following diagram illustrates the recycling of major antioxidants. The process redistributes electrons among the members of the network. Lipoic acid acts as the anchor and driving force of the antioxidant network.

BRAIN ANTIOXIDANT NETWORK

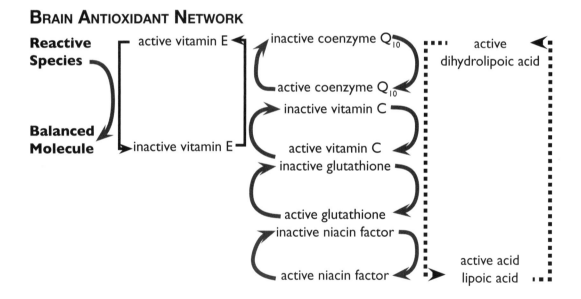

Reactive Species

Balanced Molecule

active vitamin E

inactive vitamin E

inactive coenzyme Q$_{10}$

active coenzyme Q$_{10}$

inactive vitamin C

active vitamin C

inactive glutathione

active glutathione

inactive niacin factor

active niacin factor

active dihydrolipoic acid

active acid lipoic acid

Feed your working neurons!
*Eat an array of antioxidants
from plant foods.
Use the grocery list, Chapter Five.*

Stars

Lipoic acid and carnitine

Lipoic acid

(Reduced)   (Oxidized)

Dihydrolipoic acid

Paired as alpha-lipoic acid and dihydrolipoic acid, these antioxidants are readily absorbed from the diet or supplements. The pair is also synthesized in small but significant amounts in the body, regardless of age. A. Maczurek and group studied the effects of a lipoic acid supplement, 600 mg per day, ingested for one year by a small number of patients with cognitive dementia. Cognitive functions were stabilized in the study group.

Studies of memory processing in various animal species support a mix of lipoic acid and a derivative of the peptide carnitine---*acetyl-L-carnitine*. The combination of lipoic acid with acetyl-L-carnitine has demonstrated measurable effects in spurring memory processing in very old persons with normal cognition, in any person with cognitive decline, and in individuals with early dementia. Both substances are essential ingredients in the efficient production of fuel by mitochondria.

Acetyl-L-carnitine combined with alpha-lipoic acid appears to offer some protection against the age-associated mitochondrial decay caused by oxidative stress. The combination consistently shows improved brain function and neuroprotective benefits in animal models of aging brain diseases, such as Alzheimer's and Parkinson's diseases.

Pilot studies of patients treated with acetyl-L-carnitine---in combination with folic acid, n-acetyl cysteine, the amino-acid derivative *s-adenosylmethionine* (SAM-e), and vitamins E and B-12---have demonstrated promise in interrupting the decline common in early-stage Alzheimer's disease and in slowing later stages of the disease. Amy Chan and coauthors of these studies conclude that the nutriceutical formulation may delay the onset and decline of Alzheimer's disease.

Carnitine is a peptide made primarily in the brain, liver, and kidneys from lysine and methionine (amino acids). It is considered a conditionally essential nutrient for the reduction of physical and mental fatigue in persons over seventy years of age. Cognitive improvements in young animals have also been noted with carnitine supplementation.

L-CARNITINE

The enzymes in mitochondria rapidly exchange L-carnitine and acetyl-L-carnitine. However, the acetyl format of carnitine passes more quickly into the brain and is more solidly linked to the enhancement of neurohormones against

ACETYL-L-CARNITINE

Alzheimer's. Sold as a supplement with a suggested dosage of 1.0 to 3.0 grams per day, ideal dosage or format, as L-carnitine or acetyl-L-carnitine, has not been determined. Still, the supplement has "star" potential.

Interest in alpha-lipoic acid by the scientific community as well as the public is blossoming. Prompted by the flood of retiring baby boomers, scientists are frantically exploring ways to prevent cognitive decline and salvage those golden years. With its position in the antioxidant network, alpha-lipoic acid may prove an effective aid against neurodegenerative diseases. The flexibility of lipoic acid for both fat and water-soluble compartments in a neuron, as well as its ability to regenerate other key antioxidants, makes it a potential "star." Combining alpha-lipoic acid and acetyl-L-carnitine offers neuroprotective power that certainly deserves further study in persons presenting with cognitive decline.

Vitamin E

Vitamin E is a family of eight molecules: four *tocopherols* (alpha, beta, gamma, and delta forms); and four *tocotrienols* (alpha, beta, gamma, and delta forms). Being fat-soluble, vitamin E is a "star" for the fatty brain. Neuron membranes, loaded with polyunsaturated fatty acids, are sensitive to oxidation and can be shielded by the cooperative effect of the vitamin E family. The vitamin is highly protective in the substantia nigra, a nucleus of dopamine-producing neurons noticeably decayed in early Parkinson's disease.

All members of the vitamin E family are active constituents of the antioxidant network. Tocotrienols have the same basic functions as tocopherols, but their difference in shape confers some special protective qualities for the skin and heart, over and above their antioxidant function.

VITAMIN E

Although alpha-tocopherol is the best-known form of vitamin E, supplements should contain the entire family of vitamin E isomers, labeled as *mixed tocopherols*. Better still, eat foods high in vitamin E, as suggested in Chapter Five. Then you're always swallowing the whole family of Es.

Coenzyme Q10

Ubiquinone, so called because of its ubiquitous presence in organisms, is more commonly known as coenzyme Q10. Derived from the amino acid *tyrosine*, it is produced in all animal cells, especially the heart muscle. Eighty percent of all the Q10 is concentrated in the fuel-burning mitochondria. This "star" antioxidant neutralizes reactive species and participates in energy production.

Partnering with the vitamin E family, Q10 shows promise as a treatment for Parkinson's and possibly for Alzheimer's disease. Researchers are examining the most efficient Q10 format and dosage to deter neurodegenerative diseases.

MORE
About coenzyme Q10 in Parkinson's disease

Research regarding Parkinson's has focused on the source of the disease, the *substantia nigra*. Generation of energy in the substantia nigra is compromised by excessive levels of reactive species in the mitochondria. Additionally, the DNA within the mitochondria is highly vulnerable to oxidative stress, increasing mutation and thus the risk of disease.

Levels of Q10 are depleted in the mitochondria of persons with Parkinson's. Scientists are now testing whether restoring this important antioxidant with oral supplements can alter disease progression. The National Institutes of Health agency is investing two million dollars in the trial.

Should you supplement with coenzyme Q10 to prevent or treat Parkinson's disease? Q10 is safe and well tolerated, but there is no proof of benefit to healthy people and no guidelines for use in disease prevention or treatment at this time. Dosages of 300 mg to 1.2 grams per day appear safe.

Glutathione

This is not a ho-hum antioxidant. It's a "star." Glutathione is the primary antioxidant defense in water-soluble areas of the brain and is a cofactor of antioxidant enzymes. It is a team member of the antioxidant network, regenerated by lipoic acid. It can silence the most active nitrogen species and the most damaging reactive oxygen species.

Glutathione is required by all cells. It is the brain's master antioxidant against mitochondrial aging and neurodegeneration. Glutathione has become the standard for determining redox numbers---the ratio of reduced (active) antioxidants to oxidized (inactive) antioxidants in cells---a reflection of the total antioxidant load in all cells.

glutamate   cysteine   glycine

GLUTATHIONE (REDUCED FORM)

Glutathione is produced in the liver, lungs, and brain from the amino acids cysteine, glycine, and glutamate. Swallow a supplement of glutathione and it simply breaks apart during digestion into its three component amino acids. Perhaps Little Miss Muffet found the answer to food sources of glutathione as she sat on *her tuffet eating her curds and whey*.

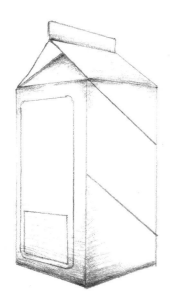

Curds and whey are the two major components of milk. Whey contains the glutathione precursor cysteine. But don't rely on cottage cheese to improve glutathione, as you have just curd, no whey.

There is a growing appreciation that milk, and in particular the milk protein whey, might prevent disease or augment conventional therapies. This is not your standard dose of milk but amounts that exceed normal dietary intakes, as in the pressurized whey bars designed to study glutathione activity. Supplements of whey or of cysteine are being evaluated for persons with cognitive decline and early Alzheimer's disease.

A direct approach to increasing glutathione in neurons is the consumption of fruits and vegetables, especially blackberries and blueberries. These fruits have the highest concentration of *polyphenols*, plant chemicals that increase the genetic expression of glutathione. Researchers studying polyphenols advise eating fruits and vegetables for more glutathione in every neuron, but not supplements of polyphenols. Again, it's food and food's direct effect on your genes.

SAM-e

The Achilles' heel in a neuron is the mitochondrial production of energy. The protective role of the antioxidant network, the proper balance of fats, adequate fuel, B-vitamins, and various minerals has been

SAM-E

discussed. A novel consideration for the aging brain is the possible limitation of SAM-e, a molecule required for metabolic reactions in the mitochondria.

Derived from the amino acid methionine, SAM-e (*s-adenosylmethionine*) is a critical factor in the metabolic functions within mitochondria, as shown in the following diagram. As neurons age and metabolism slows, the production of SAM-e by mitochondria may be less than ideal. Investigation of this mitochondrial factor as a protective factor against cognitive decline is ongoing. Preliminary observations of elderly persons given supplements of SAM-e offer promise for improved mood and enhanced efficiency of aging neurons.

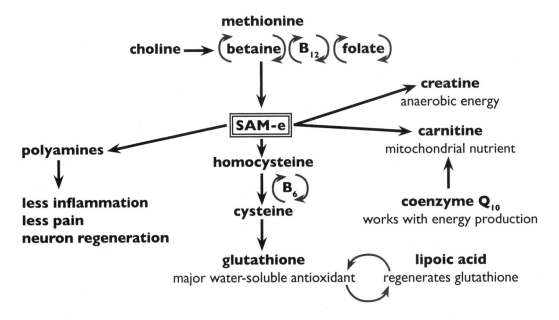

A combination of mitochondrial factors, such as SAM-e, acetyl-L-carnitine, N-acetyl cysteine, vitamin E, vitamin B-12, and folic acid are currently under investigation. The role of alpha-lipoic acid and coenzyme Q10 as mitochondrial factors in humans has yet to be extensively explored.

Are these supplements safe? The mitochondrial factors---SAM-e, carnitine, lipoic acid, coenzyme Q10, and cysteine---are made in brain cells. If the nutrient is already saturated in the neuron and you supply more, less is synthesized by the cell. Along with vitamins E, B-12, and folic acid, this is one of several mitochondrial therapies projected as helpful for persons with cognitive decline. Although considered safe, any enthusiasm for these mitochondrial supplements should be tempered with facts:

- First, there are no clinical trials validating the efficacy of supplementation with SAM-e, alpha-lipoic acid, acetyl-L-carnitive, N-acetyl cysteine, or coenzyme Q10. Since these substances are made in brain and body, a healthful diet is the first step to adequate amounts.

- Second, more studies on humans are needed to estimate the timing, mixture, and amount of supplementation helpful for a person showing signs of cognitive decline.

- Third, the doses of these substances, and others that may prove helpful, may be dramatically greater---drug levels and side effects---when treating persons with neurodegenerative disease.

- Fourth, exercise, adequate sleep, and lifestyle factors other than nutrition are necessary to retain a youthful brain.

Supplements

Some four thousand phytochemicals in food have been identified and the number grows daily. Right now, no one knows how many of them are utilized by the brain or the ideal concentration of each one. These molecules are found in fruits, flowers, roots, stems, teas, wines, grains, vegetables, herbs, and spices.

Many of the phytochemicals are antioxidants, anti-inflammatory agents, or both. The most famous antioxidants are the *carotenes*. Still, the antioxidant potency of polyphenols, a huge group of chemical compounds in fruits and vegetables, is important in glutathione synthesis and many other brain and body functions.

The first step to fixing nutrient shortfalls
is to improve food choices.
It may be that the active ingredient
in broccoli is broccoli.

---David Katz

MORE

About vitamin A

Little attention has been given to the fact that a molecule of beta-carotene can be severed into two molecules of vitamin A. Structurally, beta-carotene has antioxidant properties. Once severed in half, the format---vitamin A---no longer retains the properties of an antioxidant.

Vital for life, the functions of vitamin A in the body are essential for skeletal growth, vision, reproduction, and the maintenance of epithelial tissue. What's the role of vitamin A in the brain? The vitamin improves the efficiency of hippocampal neurons, and thus is an important contributor to memory processing and learning.

There are only a few foods high in vitamin A, but an array of plant foods are loaded with beta-carotene. The average American diet is low in fruits and vegetables, the best sources of carotenes. Getting vitamin A from foods high in beta-carotene has a triple reward: You get antioxidants from beta-carotene; carotenes regulate proteins that can go astray in Alzheimer's disease, and the liver makes vitamin A from beta-carotene as needed, without the possibility of toxicity from excess vitamin A stores in the liver.

Who needs more antioxidants? Just about everyone in the United States could use more antioxidant power, that is, from real food. The people at greatest risk are those who lack sufficient fruits and vegetables in the diet; have extensive, daily exercise regimens; are regularly exposed to environmental toxins or pollutants; consume a diet high in saturated fats, processed foods, or trans fatty acids;  experience continual emotional stress; have been diagnosed with an inflammatory disease, such as autoimmune disease, type-2 diabetes, heart disease; struggle with swings in mood; are obese. You get the idea!

We don't recommend antioxidant supplements for anyone---athlete or couch potato.

---*Wellness Letter,* University
of California, Berkeley, August 2009

From 1932 to the present, no vitamin has been the subject of more research than vitamin C. Thousands of studies have been published, at a cost of millions of dollars. Linus Pauling and his colleagues at the Linus Pauling Institute insisted that megadoses of C (3.0 grams or more per day) could prevent the common cold and cancer, among other ills.

Scientific studies have repeatedly failed to support Pauling's theories. For example, the Physicians' Health Study, reported by Howard D. Sesso and co-workers in 2008 and by J. Michael Gaziano and colleagues in 2009, verified that neither vitamin E nor vitamin C supplements reduced the risk of major cardiovascular events or cancers.

When supplements of beta-carotene increased the risk of lung cancer in smokers, antioxidants got more attention. It was found that an excess of individual antioxidants not synthesized by humans, such as carotenes, vitamin C, and vitamin E, can cause pro-oxidation---increased oxidation and decay. In 2009, Jennifer Lin and associates confirmed the lack of benefit against cancer by beta-carotene supplements, yet food sources of the antioxidant had a positive effect.

Selenium supplements may increase the risk of type-2 diabetes. Persons taking 200 mcg per day of selenium, which is about four times the recommended intake, had a fifty percent increased risk of developing diabetes as compared to those taking a placebo (*Wellness Letter*, University of California, Berkeley, December 2007). Now a large national analysis has found that excess selenium may worsen cholesterol and triglyceride levels---the supplement, not food sources (*Wellness Letter*, University of California, Berkeley, November 2008).

It is well known that oxidative stress is more severe in athletes than in sedentary individuals due to enhanced oxygen demand during exercise. *Quercetin*, one of many antioxidants from the polyphenol group, is a newly marketed supplement, with claims as the antioxidant for serious athletes.

Randi Edwards and associates reported that supplements of this antioxidant decreased blood pressure but had no effect on oxidative stress in humans. Samuel N. Cheuvront and coworkers found no effect of a quercetin supplement on endurance performance in healthy men. Research scientists warn that an excess of quercetin as a supplement may cause pro-oxidation.

Plant sources of quercetin decrease C-reactive protein concentrations and thus have proven anti-inflammatory effects in addition to antioxidant power. What foods are good sources of quercetin? Apples and berries are great choices.

> **Feed Your Working Neurons!**
> *Lifestyle and disease can destroy antioxidant power.*
> *Fill your grocery cart with antioxidant-loaded foods,*
> *as listed in Chapter Five.*

Critter Diary

Meet Shallot---a handsome goat is he! The childhood stories about goats pictured them eating old cans, nibbling on your shirt, or munching weeds in your yard. Instead, Shallot is a fussy vegetarian. He loves to eat a whole carrot---unless it has hit the ground or dropped out of someone else's mouth. That's the fussy side of Shallot.

He eats sweet potatoes, sunflower seeds, squash, and greens, and he especially loves green beans. Does he eat weeds and grasses? Sure, but flowers and tree bark are better. He is a living lesson to all of us because his diet is loaded with antioxidants.

Nutrients, a Summary

In midlife years, the work capacity and efficiency of neurons may decline, says Lauren Willis. The critical stressors damaging neurons are oxidative stress and solid fat, both boosting inflammation. Willis' group presents the latest animal studies showing that cognitive and behavioral decline can be ameliorated with polyphenols, antioxidants from fruits and vegetables, and a balance of fluid fats.

The motivation to shop, cook, eat, and enjoy fruits, vegetables, and fluid fats is generated by knowing why these nutrients are important for your neurons. The following list summarizes the neuronal nutrients discussed in this chapter. They keep your hardworking neurons toiling for you, through midlife and the years beyond, especially when neurodegeneration is knocking at your door.

SPECIAL CONSIDERATIONS FOR WORKING NEURONS

- A balance of fluid fats, 3s, 6s, 9s for power against inflammation.
- Healthful carbohydrates, consumed in their natural state, for fuel and antioxidants.
- Sufficient, lean protein, with more plant sources and fish, to synthesize mitochondrial nutrients.
- Choline and B-vitamins.
- Adequate zinc, copper, selenium, manganese, iron for antioxidant enzymes.
- A balance of potassium to sodium and calcium to magnesium for electrolyte balance.
- Vitamin C and the family of vitamin E for the antioxidant network.

When the brain lacks sufficient nutrients and micronutrients from the diet, damage is hidden---possibly for decades. If you're not sure you eat a healthful diet, vitamin-mineral supplements may appear to even the score. Jeffrey Blumberg, nutrition scientist, Tufts University, warns that supplements are no substitutes for food. He firmly believes that you can't eat a terrible diet and take supplements and think your brain is okay. The forty or so isolated micronutrients that scientists study---and supplement companies pack into capsules---are only a fraction of the array of organic compounds found in food.

Conclusion

Neurons are nutrient-greedy workaholics. The brain has always received the required load of nutrients blended and balanced in food. Don't alter a system honed for eons of time!

Brain Homework: Nutrition for a Hungry Brain:
Improve your redox number

Here's a new reason to eat correctly: Stop the decay inside working neurons. The chart on the next page presents strategies that can improve your redox number.

The factors in the left column lower your redox number, the ratio of reduced (active) antioxidants to oxidized (inactive) antioxidants. Lifestyle goals suggested on the right column improve your redox number, and thus decrease inflammation, aid in the battle against excess body fat, and protect your neurons.

FIFTEEN WAYS TO IMPROVE YOUR REDOX NUMBER

Check the factors that you need to improve and try these suggestions.

Factor: Lowers Redox Number		Goal: Improves Redox Number	
Poor daily intake of fruits & vegetables		Eat nine per day (1/2 cup per serving).	
Vigorous exercise		Exercise where/when air is clean.	
Exposure to toxic air		Filter indoor air.	
Smoke or exposure to smoker		Quit smoking; avoid smoke exposure.	
Exposure to pollutants in water		Purchase a water filter system.	
Exposure to pesticides in food		Buy organic or wash well.	
Foods with trans fat		Read label and avoid.	
Foods high in saturated fats		Choose more fish and plant foods.	
Prepackaged/processed foods		Start cooking your own meals.	
Constant emotional stress		Get help to resolve stressors.	
Chronic inflammatory disease		Seek M.D. to control inflammation.	
Heart disease		Work with lifestyle and M.D. guidelines.	
Type-2 diabetes		Control blood sugar.	
Chronic depression, anxiety		Seek treatment to normalize mood.	
Overweight or obese		First step: Stop gaining weight.	

Your Strategies:

Key References

Aliev, G., et al. Neuronal Mitochondrial Amelioration by Feeding Acetyl-L-carnitine and Lipoic Acid to Aged Rats. *Journal of Cellular and Molecular Medicine* 2009; 13(2):320-33.

Alves, E., et al. Acetyl-L-Carnitine Provides Effective In Vivo Neuroprotection over 3,4-methylenedioximetham-phetamine-induced Mitochondrial Neurotoxicity in the Adolescent Rat Brain. *Neuroscience* 2009; 158(2):514-523.

Ames, B.N., and J. Liu. Delaying the Mitochondrial Decay of Aging with Acetylcarnitine. *Annals of the New York Academy of Sciences* 2004; 1033:108-16.

Amit, Tamar, et al. Targeting Multiple Alzheimer's Disease Etiologies with Multimodal Neuroprotective and Neurorestorative Iron Chelators. *FASEB Journal* 2007; 10:1096.

Bautista-Ortega, J., et al. Egg Yolk Omega-6 and Omega-3 Fatty Acids Modify Tissue Lipid Components, Antioxidant Status, and Ex Vivo Eicosanoid Production in Chick Cardiac Tissue. *Poultry Science* 2009; 88:1167-1175.

Benson, M. K., and K. Devi. Influence of Omega-6/Omega-3 Dietary Oils on Lipid Profile and Antioxidant Enzymes in Normal and Stressed Rats. *Indian Journal of Experimental Biology* 2009; 47(2):98-103.

Blumberg, J. Jeffrey Blumberg, Ph.D: The Nutrition Agenda. *Alternative Therapy, Health, and Medicine* 2006; 12(5):64-71.

Cao, Y., et al. Comparison of Pharmacokinetics of L-carnitine, Acetyl-L-carnitine and Propionyl-L-carnitine after Single Oral Administration of L-carnitine in Healthy Volunteers. *Clinical and Investigative Medicine* 2009; 32(1):E13-E19.

Carry On, Carnitine? *Wellness Letter*, University of California, Berkeley 2009; 26(2):2-3.

Chan, Amy, et al. Efficacy of a Vitamin/Nutriceutical Formulation for Early-stage Alzheimer's Disease: A 1-year, Open-label Pilot Study with a 16-month Caregiver Extension. *American Journal of Alzheimer's Disease and Other Dementias* 2009; 23:571-585.

Cheuvront, Samuel N., et al. No Effect of Nutritional Adenosine Receptor Antagonists on Exercise Performance in the Heat. *American Journal of Physiology - Regulatory, Integrative, and Comparative Physiology* 2009; 296:R394-R401.

Coenzyme Q10: Does It Offer Hope for Parkinson's Patients? *Mind, Mood & Memory*. Massachusetts General Hospital, January 2008.

Corley, Janie, et al. Caffeine Consumption and Cognitive Function at Age 70: The Lothian Birth Cohort 1936 Study. *Psychosomatic Medicine* Feb 2010; 72:206-214.

Crivello, N. A., et al. Age- and Brain Region-specific Effects of Dietary Vitamin K on Myelin Sulfatides. *Journal of Nutrition and Biochemistry* Jan 2010, in press.

Dugan, L.L., and K.L. Quick. Reactive Oxygen Species and Aging: Evolving Questions. *Science of Aging Knowledge Environment* 2005; 2005(26):pe20.

Easlon, E., et al. The Dihydrolipoamide Acetyltransferase Is a Novel Metabolic Longevity Factor and Is Required for Calorie Restriction-mediated Life Span Extension. *Journal of Biological Chemistry* 2007; 282:6161-6171.

Edwards, Randi L., et al. Quercetin Reduces Blood Pressure in Hypertensive Subjects. *Journal of Nutrition* 2007; 137:2405-2411.

Esposito, Luke, et al. Reduction in Mitochondrial Superoxide Dismutase Modulates Alzheimer's Disease-like Pathology and Accelerates the Onset of Behavioral Changes in Human Amyloid Precursor Protein Transgenic Mice. *Journal of Neuroscience* 2006; 26:5167-5179.

Finch, Caleb E. Evolution in Health and Medicine Sackler Colloquium: Evolution of the Human Lifespan and Diseases of Aging: Roles of Infection, Inflammation, and Nutrition. *Proceedings of the National Academy of Sciences* 2010; 107:1718-1724.

Freo, U., et al. Cerebral Metabolic Effects of Acetyl-L-carnitine in Rats during Aging. *Brain Research* 2009; 1259:32-39.

Gardiner, John, et al. Neurotrophic Support and Oxidative Stress: Converging Effects in the Normal and Diseased Nervous System. *The Neuroscientist* 2009; 15:47-61.

Gaziano, J. Michael, et al. Vitamins E and C in the Prevention of Prostate and Total Cancer in Men: The Physicians' Health Study II Randomized Controlled Trial. *Journal of the American Medical Association* 2009; 301(1):52-62.

Hager, K., et al. Alpha-lipoic Acid as a New Treatment Option for Alzheimer Type Dementia. *Archives of Gerontology and Geriatrics* 2001; 32(3):275-282.

Key References (cont'd)

Halvorsen, Bente L., et al. Content of Redox-active Compounds (ie, Antioxidants) in Foods Consumed in the United States. *American Journal of Clinical Nutrition* 2006; 84(1):95-135.

Herczenik, Eszter, and Martijn F.B.G. Gebbink. Molecular and Cellular Aspects of Protein Misfolding and Disease. *FASEB Journal* 2008; 22:2115-2133.

Hindle John V. Ageing, Neurodegeneration, and Parkinson's Disease. *Age and Ageing* 2010; 39(2):156-161.

Husson, M., et al. Retinoic Acid Normalizes Nuclear Receptor Mediated Hypo-expression of Proteins Involved in Beta-amyloid Deposits in the Cerebral Cortex of Vitamin A Deprived Rats. *Neurobiology of Disease* 2006; 23(1):1-10.

Jiang, Q., et al. A Combination of Aspirin and Gamma-tocopherol Is Superior to That of Aspirin and Alpha-tocopherol in Anti-inflammatory Action and Attenuation of Aspirin-induced Adverse Effects. *Journal of Nutritional Biochemistry* 2009; 20(11):894-900.

Kidd, P.M. Neurodegeneration from Mitochondrial Insufficiency: Nutrients, Stem Cells, Growth Factors, and Prospects for Brain Rebuilding Using Integrative Management. *Alternative Medicine Review* 2005; 10(4):268-93.

Kregel, K.C., and H.J. Zhang. An Integrated View of Oxidative Stress in Aging: Basic Mechanisms, Functional Effects, and Pathological Considerations. *American Journal of Physiology - Regulatory, Integrative, and Comparative Physiology* 2007; 292:R18-R36.

Krissansen, Geoffrey W. Emerging Health Properties of Whey Proteins and Their Clinical Implications. *Journal of the American College of Nutrition* 2007; 26(6):713S-723S.

Lee, J, et al. Lower Fluid and Fruits/Vegetable Intake in Questionable Dementia among Older Hong Kong Chinese. *Journal of Nutrition in Health and Aging* Jan 2010; 14(1):45-49.

Li, Lei, et al. Supplementation with Lutein or Lutein Plus Green Tea Extracts Does Not Change Oxidative Stress in Adequately Nourished Older Adults. *Journal of Nutritional Biochemistry* 2009, in press.

Lin, Jennifer, et al. Vitamins C and E and Beta Carotene Supplementation and Cancer Risk: A Randomized Controlled Trial. *Journal of the National Cancer Institute* 2009; 101:14-23.

Linus Pauling Institute, Oregon State University. http://lpi.oregonstate.edu/infocenter (accessed 4/15/09).

Liu, J. The Effects and Mechanisms of Mitochondrial Nutrient Alpha-lipoic Acid on Improving Age-associated Mitochondrial and Cognitive Dysfunction: An Overview. *Neurochemical Research* 2008; 33(1):194-203.

Liu, J., et al. Comparison of the Effects of L-carnitine and Acetyl-L-carnitine on Carnitine Levels, Ambulatory Activity, and Oxidative Stress Biomarkers in the Brain of Old Rats. *Annals of the New York Academy of Sciences* 2004; 1033:117-31.

Liu, Jiankang, et al. Memory Loss in Old Rats Is Associated with Brain Mitochondrial Decay and RNA/DNA Oxidation: Partial Reversal by Feeding Acetyl-L-Carnitine and/or R-a-Lipoic Acid. *Proceedings of the National Academy of Sciences* 2002; 99(4):2356-2361.

Long, J., et al. Mitochondrial Decay in the Brains of Old Rats: Ameliorating Effect of Alpha-lipoic Acid and Acetyl-L-carnitine. *Neurochemical Research* 2009; 34(4):755-763.

Maczurek, A., et al. Lipoic Acid as an Anti-inflammatory and Neuroprotective Treatment for Alzheimer's Disease. *Advanced Drug Delivery Reviews* 2008; 60(13-14):1463-1470.

Malaguarnera, Mariano, et al. L-carnitine Supplementation Reduces Oxidized LDL Cholesterol in Patients with Diabetes. *American Journal of Clinical Nutrition* 2009; 89:71-77.

Malaguarnera, Mariano, et al. L-carnitine Treatment Reduces Severity of Physical and Mental Fatigue and Increases Cognitive Functions in Centenarians: A Randomized and Controlled Clinical Trial. *American Journal of Clinical Nutrition* 2007; 86:1738-1744.

McCann, Joyce C., and Bruce N. Ames. Vitamin D, an Example of Triage Theory: Is Micronutrieint Inadequacy Linked to Diseases of Aging? *American Journal of Clinical Nutrition* 2009; 90:889-907.

Milgram, N.W., et al. Acetyl-L-carnitine and Alpha-lipoic Acid Supplementation of Aged Beagle Dogs Improves Learning in Two Landmark Discrimination Tests. *FASEB Journal* 2007; 21:3756-3762.

Mischoulon, D., and M. Fava. Are Nutritional Supplements Ready for Prime Time? *Journal of Clinical Psychiatry* 2008; 69(9):1497-1498.

Key References (cont'd)

Moskaug, Jan O., et al. Polyphenols and Glutathione Synthesis Regulation. *American Journal of Clinical Nutrition* 2005; 81(1):277S-283S.

Muthian, Gladson, et al. Blockage of the Proposed Precipitating Stage for Parkinson's Disease by Antioxidants: A Potential Preventative Measure for PD. *FASEB Journal* 2008; 22:715.2.

Navarro, Ana, et al. Hippocampal Mitochondrial Dysfunction in Rat Aging. *American Journal of Physiology - Regulatory, Integrative, and Comparative Physiology* 2008; 294:R501-R509.

Oxidative Stress and Brain Disorders. Brain Briefings. http://www.sfn.org (accessed 12/15/08).

Pacher, Pal, et al. Nitric Oxide and Peroxynitrite in Health and Disease. *Physiological Reviews* 2007; 87:315-324.

Pal, R., et al. Rescue of ER Oxidoreductase Function through Polyphenolic Phytochemical Intervention: Implications for Subcellular Traffic and Neurodegenerative Disorders. *Biochemical and Biophysical Research Communication* Jan 2010, in press.

Parodi, P.W. A Role for Milk Proteins and Their Peptides in Cancer Prevention. *Current Pharmaceutical Design* 2007; 13(8):813-28.

Pfeiffer, Christine M., et al. Trends in Blood Folate and Vitamin B-12 Concentrations in the United States, 1988-2004. *American Journal of Clinical Nutrition* 2007; 86(3):718-727.

Pivik, R.T., and R.A. Dykman. Event-related Variations in Alpha Band Activity during an Attentional Task in Preadolescents: Effects of Morning Nutrition. *Clinical Neurophysiology* 2007; 18(3):615-32.

Poprzecki, S., et al. Modification of Blood Antioxidant Status and Lipid Profile in Response to High-intensity Endurance Exercise after Low Doses of Omega-3 Polyunsaturated Fatty Acids Supplementation in Healthy Volunteers. *International Journal of Food Science and Nutrition* 2009; 60 suppl 2:67-79.

Power, J.H., and P.C. Blumbergs. Cellular Glutathione Peroxidase in Human Brain: Cellular Distribution, and Its Potential Role in the Degradation of Lewy Bodies in Parkinson's Disease and Dementia with Lewy Bodies. *Acta Neuropathologica* 2009; 117(1):63-73.

Prasad, Kedar N., et al. Risk Factors for Alzheimer's Disease: Role of Multiple Antioxidants, Non-steroidal Anti-inflammatory and Cholinergic Agents Alone or in Combination in Prevention and Treatment. *Journal of the American College of Nutrition* 2002; 21(6):506-522.

Quinn, J.F., et al. Chronic Dietary Alpha-lipoic Acid Reduces Deficits in Hippocampal Memory of Aged Tg2576 Mice. *Neurobiology of Aging* 2007; 28(2):213-225.

Rebrin, I., et al. Effects of Age and Caloric Intake on Glutathione Redox State in Different Brain Regions of C57BL/6 and DBA/2 Mice. *Brain Research* 2007; 1127(1):10-18.

Ristow, Michael, et al. Antioxidants Prevent Health-promoting Effects of Physical Exercise in Humans. *Proceedings of the National Academy of Sciences* 2009; 106:8665-8670.

Schreibelt, Gerty, et al. Lipoic Acid Affects Cellular Migration into the Central Nervous System and Stabilizes Blood-brain Barrier Integrity. *Journal of Immunology* 2006; 177:2630-2637.

Sesso, Howard D., et al. Vitamins E and C in the Prevention of Cardiovascular Disease in Men: The Physicians' Health Study II Randomized Controlled Trial. *Journal of the American Medical Association* 2008; 300(18):2123-2133.

Shen, W., et al. R-alpha-lipoic Acid and Acetyl-L-carnitine Complementarily Promote Mitochondrial Biogenesis in Murine 3T3-L1 Adipocytes. *Diabetologia* 2008; 51(1):165-174.

Shenk, Justin C., et al. The Effect of Acetyl-L-carnitine and R-alpha-lipoic Acid Treatment in ApoE4 Mouse as a Model of Human Alzheimer's Disease. *Journal of the Neurological Sciences*, March 2009.

Slatore, Christopher G., et al. Long-term Use of Supplemental Multivitamins, Vitamin C, Vitamin E, and Folate Does Not Reduce the Risk of Lung Cancer. *American Journal of Respiratory and Critical Care Medicine* 2008; 177:524-530.

Smith, A., et al. Nanolipidic Particles Improve the Bioavailability and Alpha-secretase Inducing Ability of Epigallocatechin-3-gallate (EGCG) for the Treatment of Alzheimer's Disease. *International Journal of Pharmacology* Jan 2010, in press.

Sohal, Rajindar S., and Richard Weindruch. Oxidative Stress, Caloric Restriction, and Aging. *Science* 1996; 273(5271):59-63.

Key References (cont'd)

Spencer, J.P. Nutrition Society Silver Medal Lecture. Beyond Antioxidants: The Cellular and Molecular Interactions of Flavonoids and How These Underpin Their Actions on the Brain. *Proceedings of the Nutrition Society* Feb 2010, p.1-17.

Tafti, Mehdi, and Norbert B. Ghysclinck. Functional Implication of the Vitamin A Signaling Pathway in the Brain. *Archives of Neurology* 2007; 64:1706-1711.

Tarozzi, A., et al. Neuroprotective Effects of Cyanidin 3-O-glucopyranoside on Amyloid Beta (25-35) Oligomer Induced Toxicity. *Neuroscience Letter* Feb 2010, in press.

Traina, G., et al. Cytoprotective Effect of Acetyl-L-Carnitine Evidenced by Analysis of Gene Expression in the Rat Brain. *Molecular Neurobiology* 2009; 34(4):755-763.

Vedim, A., et al. Dietary Amelioration of Locomotor, Neurotransmitter, and Mitochondrial Aging. *Experimental Biology and Medicine* 2010; 235:66-76.

Vincent, Heather K., et al. Antioxidant Supplementation Lowers Exercise-induced Oxidative Stress in Young Overweight Adults. *Obesity* 2006; 14:2224-2235.

Wassef, Ramez, et al. Methionine Sulfoxide Reductase A and a Dietary Supplement S-methyl-L-cysteine Prevent Parkinson's-like Symptoms. *Journal of Neuroscience* 2007; 27:12808-12816.

Wilkins, Consuelo H., et al. Vitamin D Deficiency Is Associated with Low Mood and Worse Cognitive Performance in Older Adults. *American Journal of Geriatric Psychiatry* 2006; 14:1032-1040.

Willis, Lauren M., et al. Modulation of Cognition and Behavior in Aged Animals: Role for Antioxidant- and Essential Fatty Acid-rich Plant Foods. *American Journal of Clinical Nutrition* 2009; 89(5):1602S-1606S.

Wroth, Carmel. Simplifying Supplements. *Ode* Sept/Oct 2009, p. 43-49.

Zavorsky, G.S., et al. An Open-label Dose-response Study of Lymphocyte Glutathione Levels in Healthy Men and Women Receiving Pressurized Whey Protein Isolate Supplements. *International Journal of Food Sciences and Nutrition* 2007; 58(6):429-436.

Zhang, Hongyu, et al. Combined R-alpha-lipoic Acid and Acetyl-L-carnitine Exerts Efficient Preventative Effects in a Cellular Model of Parkinson's Disease. *Journal of Cellular and Molecular Medicine*, June 2008.

Zou, Sige, et al. Prolongevity Effects of an Oregano and Cranberry Extract Are Diet Dependent in the Mexican Fruit Fly (Anastrepha Ludens). *Journal of Gerontology Series A: Biological Science and Medical Science* 2010; 65A:41-50.

Following Chapter Five, "Resources" lists current books that may be referenced in this chapter.

THE BRAIN

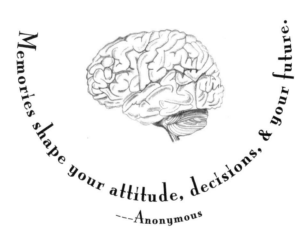

Memories shape your attitude, decisions, & your future.

---Anonymous

Chapter Five
Longevity: Nutrition
and the Prevention of Alzheimer's

Memories 150

The Science 151
    Making memories 151
    The hippocampus 153
    Place cells 155
    Memory loss 155

Firing Up Neuron Degeneration 157
    Matches for the fire 158
    Logs for the fire 159
    Aerating the fire 162

Genes and Alzheimer's Disease 166

Smart Nutrition 169
    Early action 170
    The sun vitamin 173
    Seafoods 177
    Neutralizers 179
    Daily donors 180
    Toxic mineral alert 181

Smart *Nutrition*, a Summary 183

Smart Food Choices 186

Conclusion 203

Brain Homework: A Brain-Smart Grocery List 203

Last Paragraphs 206

Key References 208

Memories

One of the intriguing functions of the brain is the ability to store information and to retrieve much of it at will. That function is called *memory*. Your cognitive power is based on learning, the process of acquiring new information. Memory is that process.

At least seventy percent of persons diagnosed with dementia in the United States have Alzheimer's disease. Worldwide, there are about twenty-six million people with this disease. The figure is projected to grow to more than one hundred six million by the year 2050. Where does the disease begin? In the hippocampus, the brain structure that processes perceptions into lasting memories.

Getting older may promise diminished capacities compared with earlier years, but thinking clearly well into later decades is a reasonable expectation. Of course, genetics plays a role. Genes may increase the chance of cognitive decline, but environmental factors remain the primary risks for most persons.

Japanese American men living in Hawaii have a higher rate of Alzheimer's disease than Japanese men living in Japan. Native Africans have significantly less Alzheimer's disease than African Americans in Indiana. Both epidemiologic findings clearly support the meaningful role of environment in aging cognition.

There are many forms of human memory: procedural, cognitive, and emotional. If you are a tennis player, procedural memory unconsciously coordinates muscles during play; your cognitive memory keeps the score; and your emotional memory recalls beating an opponent and loving it.

This chapter discusses cognitive memory, a complex process that eluded scientists for many decades. You'll follow the hippocampus as it processes a perception, see how Alzheimer's destroys the memory structures, and learn about the nutrients hailed as important deterrents of cognitive decline. Let's begin.

The Science

Today's events may be tomorrow's memories. For any memory, tomorrow may extend to a lifetime.

Making memories

In real time, perceptions are retained for about a millisecond in sensory areas of the cortex. Much of the information absorbed by your senses is then lost because it lacks personal significance. For example, you are told a telephone number. You remember that telephone number just long enough to punch it in. That's *short-term memory*.

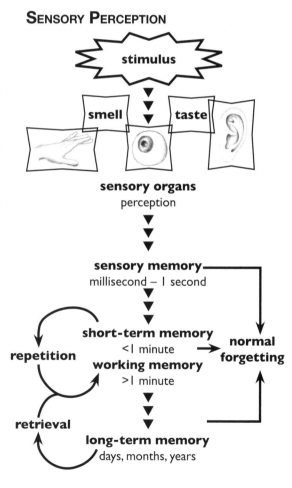

SENSORY PERCEPTION

Perhaps you want to do more---solve a math problem or ponder your next chess move. In these situations, you are working the information. The short-term memory continues to be retained as *working memory*, locked in the prefrontal cortex.

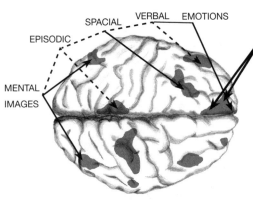

EPISODIC
SPACIAL   VERBAL   EMOTIONS
MENTAL
IMAGES

WORKING
MEMORY

Imaging studies of working memory reveal its complexity, and a number of scientists rationalize what is observed. It appears that a specific area of the prefrontal cortex may act as a *central processor* in working memory, uniting areas of the cortex to coordinate the perception. The major interacting cortical areas are the left temporal lobe, associated with the production of language and sound, and the right visual cortex, recording mental images. If the information is complex, several areas of the prefrontal cortex coordinate with the processor.

The amount of energy put into the perception is the key that opens the door to the next step, processing into *long-term memory* and learning. Information from a text, lecture, or life experience can be consolidated by the hippocampus into your personal library of facts that last a longer time---hours, days, years, or perhaps a lifetime. Your feelings regarding the facts are stored separately in the amygdala. Both facts and feelings remain linked for future retrieval.

MEMORY TOOLS

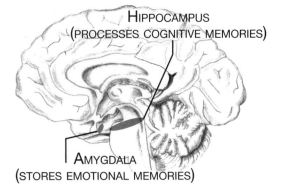

HIPPOCAMPUS
(PROCESSES COGNITIVE MEMORIES)

AMYGDALA
(STORES EMOTIONAL MEMORIES)

Intermittent challenges sharpen working memory functions in the prefrontal cortex and memory processing by the hippocampus. It's the prolonged, unresolved stress that can negatively affect brain structures.

The hippocampus

To process perceptions and facts into long-term memory, the hippocampus interacts with many of its buddies forming the *Papez's circuit*. Information travels through the hippocampus, then to the mammillary bodies of the hypothalamus, to the thalamus, to the cingulate cortex, and to the entorhinal cortex. The entorhinal

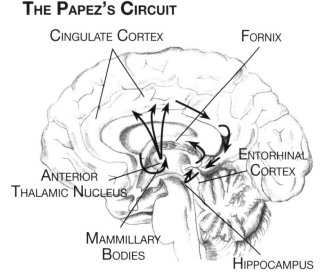

THE PAPEZ'S CIRCUIT

CINGULATE CORTEX

FORNIX

ANTERIOR THALAMIC NUCLEUS

ENTORHINAL CORTEX

MAMMILLARY BODIES

HIPPOCAMPUS

cortex exits the information back to the cortex, only to return to the hippocampus---all accomplished before you can blink.

The Papez's circuitry is repeated again and again for the same perception. When sufficiently stabilized to disengage from the hippocampus, the memory stands on its own. Similar to a puzzle, the pieces of a memory are stored in the same cortical areas from which they originated, and yet remain permanently connected.

COGNITIVE MEMORY PROCESSING   **LONG-TERM STORAGE AREAS**

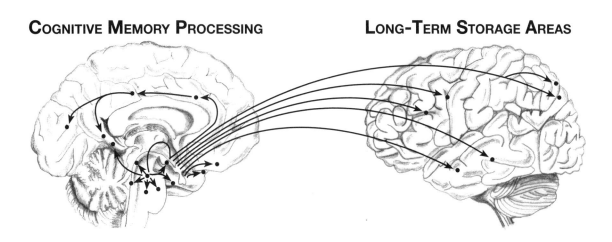

Decay of both the left and right hippocampi prevents you from learning new information. Previously stored memories, however, remain intact and can be retrieved at will.

> ### What's the Point?
> *If you were thrilled to watch Princess Diana's marriage or shocked at the sudden death of President Kennedy, probably only one pass through the Papez's circuit was needed. Both positive and negative emotions enhance memory processing.*

What you learn is a function of the energy elicited by a perception: attention, emotional state, personal interest, memories related to the perception, motivation to learn, and the context of the situation, such as the time of day, or strong odors or sounds. Retrieving a memory, talking about it, writing it down, any work with the surfaced information places it back into cortical storage areas with a greater number of linkages throughout the brain, resulting in enhanced longevity and more rapid utilization in cognitive functions. If you want the hippocampus to work for you, then work the hippocampus. Energize your brain and learning is easy at any age.

Procedural memory, the unconscious memory related to riding a bike or performing any movement, requires muscle memory, not hippocampal processing. Circuits in the cerebellum, basal ganglia, and motor cortex are modified to produce the patterns of action. Over time, you may forget important facts, but knowing how to ride a bike lasts until you no longer recognize the object as a bicycle.

PROCEDURAL MEMORY

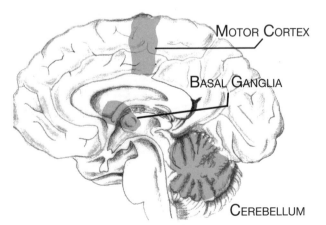

MOTOR CORTEX

BASAL GANGLIA

CEREBELLUM

Place cells

Unlike the recall of facts and events, spatial memories are processed and stored in a unique manner. The mental maps of locations are made by place cells, positioned in the CA1 region of the right hippocampus. More than a million place cells are available to store your cognitive maps.

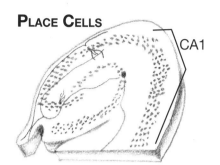

PLACE CELLS

CA1

SLICE OF RIGHT HIPPOCAMPUS

Explore a new environment and place cells map the area into a memory that can be stable for months, even without reinforcement. In the early stage of Alzheimer's disease, neuron loss is concentrated in the CA1 area of the hippocampus. If you relocate a person with early disease, the place cells may not map the new residence, and the person gets lost easily.

Place cells also retrieve information in a sequence of time or space. A biography is organized in the correct sequence of years, days, or perhaps even minutes with the aid of your place cells.

Memory loss

Memory loss is not necessarily the beginning stage of Alzheimer's disease. Memories fade because they are, at the molecular level, proteins. Proteins lose their shape and become nonfunctional over time. A good example of memory loss is vocabulary. If you have not retrieved a word in a long time, connections weaken. It takes longer to recall the term or remember its meaning. In this case, use what has been learned or you lose the memory, regardless of age.

In contrast, the processing of information into new memories is particularly vulnerable to decline as you age. By midlife, memory processing may be noticeably less efficient. Why? The hippocampus and associated areas of memory storage in the cortex contain tightly packed specialty neurons that capture and save perceptions---*pyramidal neurons.* Their shape resembles a pyramid.

PYRAMIDAL NEURON

Pyramidal neurons are extremely sensitive to oxygen and glucose deprivation. After decades of an unhealthful lifestyle---eating too much sugar or saturated and trans fats, stressing over challenges in your life, living in a sleep-deprived state---it's no surprise that your arteries narrow and the flow of oxygen and glucose to neurons becomes inadequate. High blood pressure just adds another dimension to pyramidal starvation.

If untreated, negative moods cause a surge of cortisol, notably toxic to pyramidal neurons. Eventually, pyramidal neurons, extending throughout the neocortex, may be unable to integrate thoughts, feelings, and memories into rational decisions---a sign of dementia.

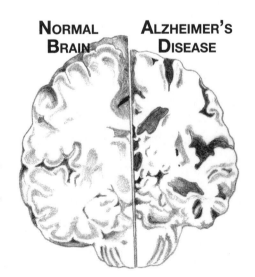

NORMAL BRAIN   **ALZHEIMER'S DISEASE**

Look out for lax middle years. Unhealthful habits are silently affecting the risk of cognitive decline, and possibly late-life dementia, in a dose-dependent manner.

Firing Up Neuron Degeneration

There is clear evidence linking chronic inflammation, increased cytokine formation, and neurodegeneration.

---Mark DeLegge

GLUTAMATE TOXICITY

GLUTAMATE

CYTOKINES (INFLAMMATORY PROTEINS)

CYTOCHROME C

MITOCHONDRIA DESTROYED

CYTOCHROME C RELEASED BY MITOCHONDRIA

PHAGOCYTOSIS

NEURON DEATH

Scattered throughout the hippocampus are neurons that release the most excitatory neurochemical in the brain---*glutamate*. Similar to a recipe that needs a pinch of hot pepper sauce, glutamate adds a burst of energy for quick processing of a perception into a long-term memory.

If the hippocampal cells begin to atrophy, as in Alzheimer's disease, the glutamate stored in these neurons is randomly released into the brain, triggering neurons into a state of hyperexcitability. Uncontrolled, the excitable state is toxic to brain cells. Neuronal decay signals an inflammatory response.

This is not a classic inflammation. Neuroinflammation causes no heat, redness, pain, or swelling. It is a silent process that may be reflected by a highly sensitive C-reactive protein test.

What's the Point?
Forgetting where you put your car keys is normal. When you don't know the function of a key, that's dementia.

Robert Stewart and co-workers recorded blood levels of C-reactive protein in Japanese American men for twenty-five years. Men with the highest values had a threefold increased risk for all dementias, but mainly Alzheimer's disease and vascular dementia. C-reactive protein was elevated long before clinical symptoms of disease appeared and may thus be an early marker for dementia. In fact, some researchers believe that amyloid plaques are simply the victims of too much inflammatory activity in the brain.

Chronic neuroinflammation simmers
like the pot on a low flame that
is unnoticed until the pot burns.

---Patrick McGeer

The role of inflammation in dementia is supported by epidemiological data. When doctors treating Alzheimer's patients took a close look at who seemed to be succumbing to the disease, they uncovered a tantalizing clue: Persons already taking anti-inflammatory drugs for arthritis or heart disease tended to develop Alzheimer's disease later than those who weren't.

Matches for the fire

GLIAL CELL

The brain lesions associated with Alzheimer's disease
are characterized by the presence
of a broad spectrum of inflammatory mediators,
produced by resident brain cells.

---Federico Licastro

The most likely inflammatory culprits in the brain are glial cells. Known to nourish neurons, glial cells also monitor the environment around neurons. When there is a metabolic need for an inflammatory response, the glial cells release inflammatory cytokines. In Alzheimer's disease, chronic glial cell activation is observed and inflammation appears uncontrolled.

MORE

About glial cells and inflammation

Of all glial cells, the astrocyte is the primary cell contributing to inflammation. Mechanisms that trigger astrocyte activation are now being explored. A protein called *calcineurin* has been linked to astrocyte activation. This protein regulates inflammatory-signaling pathways.

Chemicals that block calcineurin activity might become the anti-inflammatory medications of the future. Once activated, astrocytes produce prostaglandins and cytokines. As discussed in Chapter Three, the nature of the prostaglandin, pro- or anti-inflammatory, depends on your intake of omega-3 and omega-6 fatty acids.

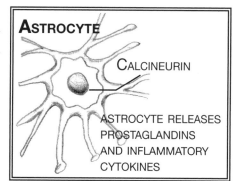

ASTROCYTE

CALCINEURIN

ASTROCYTE RELEASES PROSTAGLANDINS AND INFLAMMATORY CYTOKINES

Logs for the fire

Although the future holds promise for early diagnosis, Alzheimer's is presently diagnosed *definitively* upon autopsy.

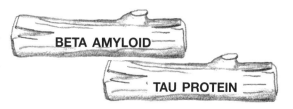

BETA AMYLOID

TAU PROTEIN

The brain disease is characterized by the precipitation and unmanageable accumulation of distinct proteins---*tangles* and *plaques*---over time. Like adding logs to a fire, tangles and plaques escalate inflammation in the hippocampus.

V.P. Reddy and co-workers hypothesize that oxidative stress and inflammation are causal for Alzheimer's disease, while the precipitated proteins are the effect. Regardless, the logs (distinct proteins) are present, interfere with neuron function, and thus lead to neuron atrophy.

The assumed disease scenario begins with neurons secreting a healthful protein (*amyloid precursor protein*) into the intercellular fluid. The protein is neuroprotective, triggered into production when the neuron is subjected to stress or injury.

Once produced, enzymes known as *secretases* break the amyloid precursor protein into segments. Beta-amyloid fragments (peptides) hover around the hippocampus and assist in memory processing, learning, and the genesis of new hippocampal neurons.

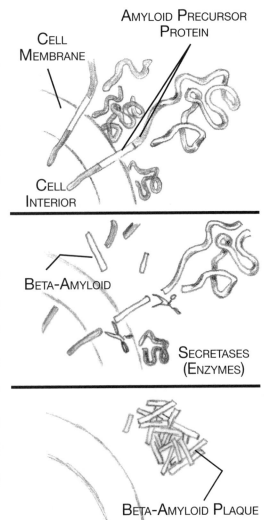

The beta fragments (peptides) of the precursor protein, composed of forty-two amino acids, are the least soluble of the peptides and the most commonly identified around the hippocampus. Over time, mild oxidation and inflammation in the brain cause clumping of these amyloid fragments, primarily on the outer surface of hippocampal neurons.

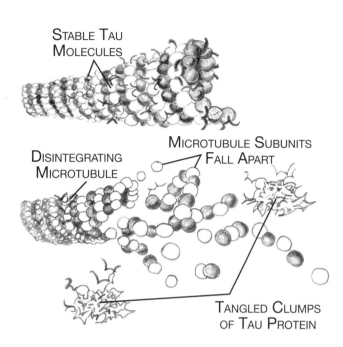

STABLE TAU MOLECULES

DISINTEGRATING MICROTUBULE

MICROTUBULE SUBUNITS FALL APART

TANGLED CLUMPS OF TAU PROTEIN

The debris disturbs the flow of ions in and out of the neuron membrane. With the neuron's source of energy partially disrupted, oxidative stress rises and components within the neuron body begin to decay. Astrocytes, the glial cells that normally nourish neurons, now release inflammatory cytokines, further weakening neurons and escalating plaque formation.

In Alzheimer's disease, *tau proteins* that maintain the structural integrity of small tubules within the neuron react with phosphorus, lose their capacity to bind to the microtubules, and knot into tangles. The weakened hippocampal neurons are now susceptible to attack by the brain's immune cells called *microglia*.

The hippocampus shrinks. Eventually, new memories can no longer be processed. All neurons associated with memory processing and memory storage---the entire cortex---decays.

ALZHEIMER'S DISEASE: INITIAL SITES OF DECAY

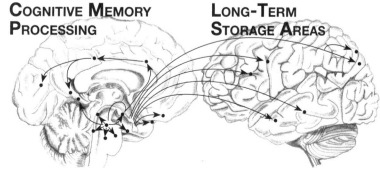

COGNITIVE MEMORY PROCESSING

LONG-TERM STORAGE AREAS

Aerating the fire

*If there is inflammation anywhere
in brain or body,
there is inflammation everywhere.*

---Patrick McGeer

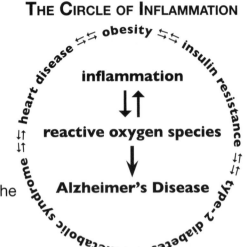

THE CIRCLE OF INFLAMMATION

obesity
heart disease
insulin resistance
inflammation
⬇⬆
reactive oxygen species
⬇
Alzheimer's Disease
type-2 diabetes
metabolic syndrome

Untreated, uncontrolled diseases add fuel to the fire labeled inflammation.

The heart

Recent advances in basic science have established inflammation as the mediator of every step leading to atherosclerosis. The standard marker is C-reactive protein.

*Inflammation is the alpha
and omega of atherosclerosis.*

---Peter Libby

Blood cholesterol parameters are major indicators of arterial closure. Yet half of all heart attacks occur in people with normal values. Twenty-five to thirty million Americans fall into the low cholesterol/high C-reactive protein category. The conclusion: Inflammation in the cardiovascular system affects neuronal inflammation.

> **Heart disease hint:**
> *Add omega-3s, eat lean proteins, and learn to manage stressors.*

The relationship between Alzheimer's disease and cardiovascular risk factors has led many researchers to consider Alzheimer's as a vascular disease. Narrowing of cerebral vessels can lead to shrinkage of the brain. When medication improves cardiovascular functions, it also improves Alzheimer's symptoms. By changing modifiable vascular risk factors, there is emerging evidence that it may be possible to prevent or delay dementia. The health of your heart is meaningful for your brain.

Blood sugar

Hyperglycemia induces an inflammatory response in the endothelial cells of the blood-brain barrier and may disrupt the barrier. In a study of thousands of Swedish twins with hyperglycemia, the twin who developed type-2 diabetes before age sixty-five had a 125 percent increased risk of Alzheimer's disease as compared to the twin sibling without diabetes. The conclusion: Nutrition matters. Hyperglycemia-induced oxidative stress in the brain makes antioxidants a necessity, not an option, to curb inflammation.

> **Blood sugar hint:**
> *Eat more legumes, especially chickpeas,*
> *and antioxidants in low-calorie fruits and vegetables.*

How does excess glucose contribute to inflammation? Glucose and other sugar molecules react with proteins to form *advanced glycation end products*. Glucose bound to proteins in the lens of the eye can lead to cataracts. The end products that attach to receptors on neuron membranes create reactive oxygen species and inflammation. The conclusion: Activated glycation end products stabilize beta-amyloid plaques.

Body fat, belly fat

Chronically enlarged fat cells release the inflammatory cytokine, tissue necrosis factor-alpha. Now put those enlarged adipocytes in the belly around abdominal organs and you've got trouble. The conclusion: Health issues, including, but not limited to, insulin resistance, type-2 diabetes, cardiovascular disease, and Alzheimer's disease skyrocket in the presence of belly fat.

> **Belly fat hint:** *Eat smaller portions, decrease alcohol consumption, lose weight and keep it off.*

What happens when you have significant cardiovascular risk factors, type-2 diabetes, and belly fat? You're categorized as having metabolic syndrome. Although metabolic syndrome was previously considered an aging problem, the prevalence and severity of childhood and adolescent obesity in the United States have increased dramatically over the past three decades. It is estimated that more than forty million persons will be affected by metabolic syndrome, and belly fat is a determining factor.

Insulin dysfunction

Insulin resistance is associated with an increased risk for Alzheimer's disease.

---J. M. Burns

NORMAL INSULIN METABOLISM

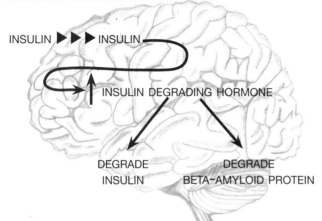

INSULIN ▶ ▶ ▶ INSULIN

INSULIN DEGRADING HORMONE

DEGRADE INSULIN

DEGRADE BETA-AMYLOID PROTEIN

INSULIN DYSFUNCTION

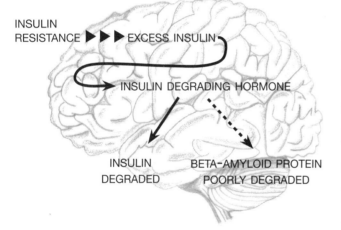

INSULIN RESISTANCE ▶ ▶ ▶ EXCESS INSULIN

INSULIN DEGRADING HORMONE

INSULIN DEGRADED

BETA-AMYLOID PROTEIN POORLY DEGRADED

Decades ago insulin was identified in the brain. With the blood-brain barrier supposedly impervious to proteins such as insulin, it was hypothesized that the brain synthesized its own insulin. Over time, the facts emerged. The barrier houses a special transporter for insulin. Little if any insulin is produced by neurons.

Insulin plays a positive role in brain function. The hormone stimulates the release of an *insulin denaturing enzyme*. This enzyme preferentially degrades insulin but also regulates amyloid proteins. With hyperinsulinemia, the enzyme becomes saturated with insulin molecules. The breakdown and removal of beta-amyloid proteins are sacrificed. Beta-amyloid plaques collect and inflammation soars. The conclusion: Insulin resistance is the result of peripheral inflammation and a cause of brain inflammation.

Insulin dysfunction hint: *Exercise regularly, get enough sleep, and eat whole foods---especially legumes.*

Over time, insulin resistance contributes to the expression of Alzheimer's disease, vascular dementia, Parkinson's disease, and other neurodegenerative diseases. Yet if persons with both insulin resistance and mild Alzheimer's disease are given drugs that improve insulin sensitivity, they have better memory function after just four months of treatment. The brain truly responds to a positive environment---less insulin, less inflammation.

Other aerators

Wherever there is inflammation, put it out! Steven Shoelson, associate director of research at the Joslin Diabetes Center, produced the entire constellation of metabolic syndrome in mice (this includes cardiovascular factors, diabetes, and visceral obesity) just by inciting inflammation.

> **Hint:** *Decrease the amount of sugar and refined grains in your diet.*

A long-term bacterial infection, such as periodontal disease, keeps the internal fires burning and tips the balance toward chronic inflammation. Unresolved mood disorders, asthma, chronic infections, rheumatoid arthritis, and other autoimmune diseases aerate internal fires and attack the brain. The inflammatory proteins circulating in the body---tumor necrosis factor-alpha and other cytokines---send impulses to the brain via the vagus nerve. These inflammatory proteins are then synthesized in the brain. The conclusion: Any chronic inflammation increases the risk of cognitive decline.

Genes and Alzheimer's Disease

Alzheimer's disease is divided into two formats: genetically inherited disease, known as *familial*; and the format showing no clear inheritance pattern, *sporadic*.

ALZHEIMER'S DISEASE

FAMILIAL	SPORADIC
early onset	late onset
rare	common
onset age 30-60	onset ages 65-90
three genes identified	unknown number of recessive genes
increased beta-amyloid production	impaired clearance of beta-amyloid proteins
increased plaques early in life	tendency toward inflammation
role of nutrition unknown	Anti-inflammatory nutrients, antioxidants, plus other lifestyle factors alter risk. Mitochondrial nutrients may support the efficiency of the aging brain.

Sporadic Alzheimer's disease is the late-onset format. It typically affects only two percent of individuals age sixty-five, with the incidence roughly doubling every five years. Scientists studying the genetics of Alzheimer's have found that the mutations seen in early-onset are not involved in sporadic disease. What causes some, but not all, persons to accumulate plaques and tangles in sufficient numbers to result in late-onset disease? The presence of subtle, genetic differences, called *polymorphisms*, is a factor.

Although a specific gene has not been identified as the cause of late-onset Alzheimer's disease, one predisposing genetic factor, the apolipoprotein E gene (ApoE), contains the instructions needed to make a protein that carries cholesterol in the bloodstream. ApoE comes in several different forms, or *alleles*. You inherit one copy of the gene from each parent. Three forms---ApoE2, ApoE3, and ApoE4---occur most frequently and appear to influence the age at which the disease may occur.

ApoE2 is relatively rare and seems to offer some protection against the disease. If Alzheimer's disease does occur in a person with this allele, it develops later in life than it would in someone with the ApoE4 gene. ApoE3 is the most common allele, playing a neutral role in Alzheimer's disease---neither decreasing nor increasing risk. ApoE4 occurs in about forty percent of all people who develop late-onset disease and is present in about twenty-five to thirty percent of the population.

People with Alzheimer's disease are more likely to have an ApoE4 allele than people who do not develop the disease. However, inheriting an ApoE4 allele does not mean that a person will definitely develop Alzheimer's. Some people with one or two ApoE4 alleles never get the disease, and others who develop the disease don't have ApoE4 alleles.

Dozens of studies have confirmed that the ApoE4 allele increases the risk of developing Alzheimer's disease, but the mechanism is not yet understood. It appears that Alzheimer's is more likely when the ApoE and other polymorphic genes you inherit favor increased expression of pro-inflammatory mediators or decreased expression of anti-inflammatory mediators. Patients with late-onset disease generally express fewer anti-inflammatory mediators.

Polymorphisms related to inflammation are fairly common in the general population. There is a likelihood that anyone will inherit one or more of these alleles, reflecting a tendency toward inflammation. Remember, lifestyle factors can alter inflammation. Anti-inflammatory factors and antioxidants in plant food, stress management, exercise, sufficient sleep---these healthful habits cripple the expression of polymorphic genes that are inflammatory prone.

The risk for sporadic Alzheimer's disease is modified by genes other than ApoE4. The protein coded by the GAB2 gene was suspected to slow Alzheimer's progression in persons with the ApoE4 gene, reported by M. Arfan Ikram and staff. R. Ramirez-Lorca and coworkers studied persons in Spain with Alzheimer's. Their results did not support the association of the GAB2 gene as a disease modifier.

Another risk factor is the gene SORL1, coding for the protein *sortilin-related receptor*. This receptor is implicated in the uptake of ApoE proteins throughout the body and brain. The gene product also affects beta-amyloid protein in the brain. When SORL1 is present at low levels or in a variant form, beta-amyloid accumulates, and the ensuing precipitation harms neurons. The available data support a role for SORL1 in sporadic Alzheimer's.

Scientists believe that four to seven genes affect the risk of Alzheimer's disease. It's time to defend your brain against cognitive decline and Alzheimer's disease. The next section, "Smart Nutrition," presents nutrients that add protection against inflammation and neurodegenerative disease.

Genes do not determine disease on their own. Nutrition plays a critical role in determining which genes, good and bad, are expressed.

---Colin T. Campbell

Smart Nutrition

In the spring of 1907, an autopsy by Dr. Alois Alzheimer identified lesions in the brain of his patient. Her disease was called Alzheimer's. A century later, the patient's haunting words, "I have lost myself," still define the disease.

Early action

The primary focus of research funded by the National Institutes of Health is the transitional stage between normal memory loss and mild Alzheimer's disease, called *amnestic mild cognitive impairment*. According to scientists at Massachusetts General Hospital, the number of persons with cognitive impairment was growing much more rapidly than expected---about five percent a year rather than one to two percent---until 2008. The risk of progression to dementia from cognitive impairment declined about one-third the expected number in 2008. Lifestyle intervention is making a difference. Good news!

Clear differences are observed in the brains of persons with normal aging changes, those with amnestic mild cognitive impairment, and those diagnosed with mild Alzheimer's disease. A person with mild cognitive impairment has eighteen percent fewer synapses than someone with normal cognition, while anyone with mild Alzheimer's disease has fifty-five percent fewer synapses, according to S. W. Scheff and coworkers. The number of synapses is an indication of networking, a protective feature of a brain resistant to disease.

Persons with mild cognitive impairment may progress to different types of dementia, stay stable, or even improve. A Canadian study by J. D. Fisk and K. Rockwood found that twenty to thirty percent of patients diagnosed with cognitive impairment were normalized at a five-year follow-up---if treatment was aggressive.

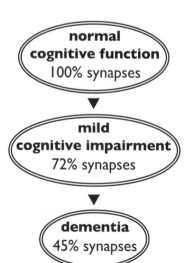

Neurodegeneration is not inevitable. When impaired, the brain actively attempts to normalize:

- Early neurodegenerative changes are correlated with increased production of acetylcholine, the neurotransmitter required for the processing and storage of a memory.
- The greater activity of serotonin observed in patients with mild cognitive impairment sparks brain-derived hormones to repair the hippocampus.

By the time mild Alzheimer's disease is reached, however, the brain has terminated any observable attempts at repair. The conclusion: Early diagnosis is crucial and nutrient defenses for neurons is just plain smart.

MORE

About early detection

The drums are beating in the media and among some researchers for universal screening of dementia, beginning as early as age fifty. Many community groups offer memory tests. Some doctors routinely evaluate patients over age sixty-five, usually with questionnaires. Would you be better off if Alzheimer's could be diagnosed early? This is a subject of continuing controversy.

A general characteristic of persons with cognitive impairment is the rapid decay of *iconic* memory, a recall of visual perceptions two to three seconds after an observation. *Echoic* memory tests, recalling what was heard two to three seconds after recognizing sounds, can also point to cognitive impairment.

Still, people have a wide range of memory problems, not all of them leading to dementia. The Alzheimer's Association recommends a thorough medical examination, including cognitive examinations administered by a trained health professional. Objective evaluations of tests by the United States Preventive Services Task Force find the evidence for accuracy and benefits of self-testing insufficient and recommend avoiding them.

Brain imagery provides insight into the trajectory of aging and dementia. Time-lapse images show a rapidly advancing wave of cortical atrophy sweeping from hippocampal structures into cognitive and sensorimotor areas of the brain. The pattern correlates with the cognitive decline clinically observed in Alzheimer's patients but does not offer a definitive diagnosis.

Volumetric magnetic resonance imaging (MRI) analysis of the hippocampus is a promising new technology, and novel positron emission tomography imaging tracers can spot disease early. New satellite-intelligent technology helps to distinguish between Alzheimer's disease and mild cognitive impairment in magnetic resonance images. But what's the cost?

New research suggests that cognitive decline may be associated with higher risk for age-related macular degeneration, a form of vision impairment characterized by loss of ability to see objects in the center of the visual field. Similarly, persons who have macular degeneration tend to score poorly on cognitive tests. Currently in clinical studies, a new test evaluates amyloid proteins in the eye using fluorescent antibodies to the protein. The amyloid protein is present in the eye long before any clinical signs of Alzheimer's---an early warning.

Probable diagnosis is made in the living patient with at least eighty-five percent accuracy, using a combination of cognitive testing by trained professionals and a thorough medical examination to exclude conditions that may appear as pseudodementias, such as depression, hypothyroidism, and vitamin B-12 deficiency.

Upon autopsy, Alzheimer's disease is officially diagnosed by the presence of unique beta-amyloid lesions. There is, however, a possibility of error in the diagnosis. As the brain ages, some accumulation of beta-amyloid plaques is inevitable. The presence of plaques in the brain is not sufficient evidence for the diagnosis of disease. Cognitive training enhances the processing of information, in spite of some debris around neurons. Beta-amyloid plaques may be noted by pathologists, yet clinical symptoms of disease not observed by caregivers or the attending physician.

The sun vitamin

Vitamin D is the big buzz these days. Americans have significantly lower blood levels of vitamin D than they had ten to fifteen years ago---less sun, less milk. There are receptors for vitamin D everywhere, not just on bone cells. The vitamin has been reported as especially important for the prevention of colon cancer, breast cancer, cardiovascular disease, osteoporosis, and type-2 diabetes. The mechanism of protection is linked to the anti-inflammatory effects of the vitamin.

Vitamin D is also smart nutrition for the brain. Receptors for the vitamin are numerous in the hippocampus. As far back as 1998, chronic treatment of rats with the sun vitamin retarded age-related atrophy in hippocampal neurons. Fast-forward to 2009 and the data show that aging persons with the lowest vitamin D levels have double the risk of cognitive impairment. The vitamin may also play a role in improving depression, as this mood disorder is directly related to poor hippocampal functioning.

The omega-3/omega-6 ratio is just partly responsible for balancing inflammation. Vitamin D is an important protectant against inflammation and oxidative decay in the brain. Food sources currently hold little promise of meeting the vitamin D need for 1,000 IU or more per day. For example, a serving of wild salmon has 360 IU; farmed salmon, 90 IU; sardines, 250 IU; milk, 98 IU; margarine, 60 IU; cereal, 40 IU; egg, 20 IU. Food technologists are hoping vitamin-D-enhanced mushrooms may boost the intake of the vitamin.

MORE
About vitamin D

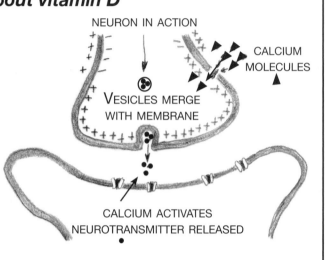

NEURON IN ACTION

CALCIUM MOLECULES

VESICLES MERGE WITH MEMBRANE

CALCIUM ACTIVATES NEUROTRANSMITTER RELEASED

Balancing calcium is well recognized as an important function in controlling the loss of neurons. The hippocampus is especially sensitive to excitability by calcium ions. The active metabolite of vitamin D, 1,25-dihydroxyvitamin D-3, is the major steroid hormone balancing calcium activity in the hippocampus and the brain in general.

Joyce McCann and Bruce N. Ames published a review of the evidence linking vitamin D deficiency to brain dysfunction. They concluded that the vitamin is critical to early brain development as well as lifelong protection against inflammation and neurodegeneration.

According to research at the Harvard School of Public Health, vitamin D may ward off multiple sclerosis, one of the most common neurological diseases in young adults. Researchers found that persons with the highest levels of vitamin D had the lowest risks for multiple sclerosis. Still, don't count out the role of gender and heredity in the incidence of this disease.

Vitamin D's ever-expanding benefits may include an effect on Parkinson's disease. Lower levels of the vitamin in persons with Parkinson's compared to those with Alzheimer's hints of a link between Parkinson's and the sun vitamin. C. H. Wilkins and group looked at vitamin D deficiencies in older adults and found both low mood and cognitive impairment. Sunlight is a stimulant for the production of serotonin---related to mood---not just vitamin D. Sunny days bring better moods, better bones, better brain protection---and who knows what more will be discovered?

The Centers for Disease Control and Prevention estimates that as many as 75 percent of Americans have a low blood level of vitamin D. Sun exposure is the principal source of vitamin D. Sunlight is great for the health of the brain, but not so good for the skin. Only ten to fifteen minutes of direct sun exposure is recommended daily. If you prefer to bring the sun indoors, you'll need a medium-pressure lamp that emits the UVB rays the body uses in making vitamin D, such as the lamp approved by the U.S. Food and Drug Agency. Tanning salons use only high-pressure lamps that produce UVA light.

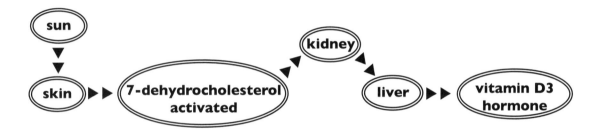

The amount of vitamin D generated by the sun depends on the time of day, the season, your distance from the equator, your exposure to the sun, and your use of sunscreen or sunblock. With identical environments, persons with dark skin pigmentation make less vitamin D than light-skinned individuals. As you age, less vitamin D is produced from sun exposure in any environment. High-risk persons are nursing infants, the elderly, and African Americans of all ages. Even if you live in the sunbelt, you can still be deficient in vitamin D.

Based on unproved assumptions, ingesting large amounts of this fat-soluble vitamin---as a supplement---has been considered harmful. No adverse effects have yet been noted from intakes as high as 10,000 IU of vitamin D per day, yet even 1,000 IU are impossible to achieve through food and safe sun exposure.

What's the Point?
Is your vitamin D level adequate?
Although the procedure is pricey
and may not be covered by
insurance, serum vitamin D
can be measured.

The normal value
for vitamin D varies from state to
state, but the range is generally
30-50 ng/ml. Lower readings (25
ng/ml) in the late winter and early
spring are acceptable. Persons with
vitamin D values below the standard
are prescribed a high dose of the
vitamin until the value normalizes.

Obesity presents an additional concern. A fat-soluble chemical, vitamin D is stored in adipose tissue. As body fat increases, less vitamin D is available for neuronal needs. It's called *fat sequestration*. As your body fat increases, your intake of vitamin D may need to be increased.

Because vitamin D is currently under investigation and benefits may be identified for your heart, retina, brain, and tissues other than bone, it is best to keep abreast of new recommendations as they emerge. Review your vitamin D status and personal health needs with your attending physician on a regular basis.

The Institute of Medicine warns that prolonged supplementation with 20,000 IU of vitamin D may affect blood levels of calcium and blood pressure, and may cause nausea, weakness, constipation, or kidney damage. Meanwhile, supplementation escalates.

Supplements of vitamin D have two formats: vitamin D-3 or *cholecalciferol*, the natural form produced by skin exposure to sunlight and the format in food; and vitamin D-2 or *ergocalciferol*, isolated from fungi exposed to ultraviolet light. Although both D-2 and D-3 are converted into the same active hormone, the D-3 format is longer acting and about three times more potent than D-2.

Look for vitamin D-3 (cholecalciferol) on the label of supplements and fortified foods. Check the list of ingredients and avoid fish liver oil as a source of vitamin D unless you know the product is free of mercury and low in vitamin A. Store fish oil in a dark bottle and keep it in the refrigerator to prevent rancidity.

Seafoods

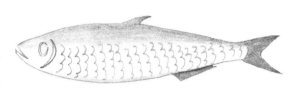

Long-term use of non-steroidal, anti-inflammatory drugs may be a tempting solution for neuroprotection, but these drugs, consumed long-term, can have serious side effects. Anti-inflammatory nutrients have no therapeutic risk. In a review of the scientific literature from 2008 through July 2009, the data show that dietary intake of omega-3s or fish decreased dementia risk of animals and humans in nineteen of the twenty-two studies reported. It's smart nutrition.

May A. Beydoun reported that promoting higher intakes of omega-3s in the diet of persons with high blood pressure and elevated LDLs may have substantial benefits in reducing the risk of decline in verbal fluency. The right fats may protect the head even when the cardiovascular system is not performing properly.

Jyrki Virtanen and colleagues found that omega-3s prevent brain infarcts, small areas of tissue that die from an insufficient blood supply. The infarct is called "silent," showing no obvious symptoms, but it is associated with the risk of stroke as well as cognitive impairment, and possibly Alzheimer's disease.

Keep your brain loaded with omega-3s to suppress inflammation and enhance the structural stability of neurons. Eat two to three servings of fish per week.

How much fish oil? Results from the Framingham Heart Study suggest that consuming one gram of fish oil daily is associated with a fifty percent reduction in dementia. Medical sources recommend one to two grams of fish oil daily.

Currently, Swedish scientists are testing the safety and tolerability of four grams of fish oil per day as a therapeutic dose for mild to moderate Alzheimer's disease. Two other double-blind, placebo-controlled clinical studies are underway to evaluate whether omega-3s are effective in treating patients with mild disease. These exciting clinical studies are attempting to maximize the power of nutrition against Alzheimer's.

In 2010, researchers will launch the VITAL Trial, a study combining vitamin D-3 and omega-3s. The group will evaluate whether 2,000 IUs a day of vitamin D-3 and 1,000 mg a day total of EPA and DHA can lower the risk of cancer, heart disease, stroke, neurodegeneration, age-related blindness, and other illnesses. For more information: www.vitalstudy.org.

MORE
About DHA

The omega-3 fatty acid, DHA, stabilizes neuron membranes, but how does DHA act against Alzheimer's disease? Recent nuclear magnetic resonance studies directly confirm that increasing brain DHA can modify processing pathways in neuron membranes and decrease the generation of amyloid protein.

DHA is converted into a protectin called *neuroprotectin D-1*. This novel DHA-derived compound thus shields against the precipitation of beta-amyloid proteins into plaques. The concentration of both DHA and neuroprotectin D-1 is low in the hippocampi of patients with Alzheimer's disease.

In the Framingham Heart Study, persons in the top 25 percent of plasma DHA level were associated with a forty-seven percent reduction in the risk of developing all-cause dementia. According to O. van de Rest and co-workers' report of the Zutphen Elderly Study, both DHA and EPA retarded the decline in cognition.

Once neuron membranes are formed, can you significantly change their DHA content? F. Calon reported brain DHA levels were reduced sixteen percent with DHA-depleted diets. Giselle P. Lim showed that DHA supplementation enhanced DHA in neuron membranes and reversed some insoluble amyloid plaques in aged mice. You do become what you eat---eventually.

Neutralizers

As oxidative stress rises in the mitochondria of hippocampal neurons, so should the number of antioxidants you consume in food. Antioxidants are part of the complex world of organic chemicals acting as peacemakers in the molecular war against oxidation and inflammation.

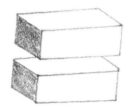

The data are strong for the preventive role of antioxidants in fruits and vegetables against Alzheimer's disease. The work of antioxidants is not always good news when humans interfere with the natural environment by taking antioxidant supplements.

Under some circumstances, antioxidants can turn into pro-oxidants and promote oxidative stress, seen only with the use of supplements. Read the section "Smart Food Choices" for information about individual foods loaded with antioxidants.

Daily donors

 A nasty little amino acid can clog blood vessels, provide kindling for inflammation, and contribute to cognitive impairment. Meant to exist for milliseconds, *homocysteine* has a well-deserved reputation as a neurotoxin. An excess of homocysteine in the blood may disrupt the blood-brain barrier and increase the risk of dementia.

Homocysteine impairs the action of growth factors important to the repair and maintenance of the hippocampus. Researchers in Ireland reported that higher levels of homocysteine were consistently associated with poor performance in tests assessing visual memory and verbal recall.

Homocysteine levels are strongly influenced by genetics. Still, gene expression is altered by lifestyle factors. The metabolic steps required to break down homocysteine are illustrated in the diagram.

HOMOCYSTEINE METABOLISM

methionine

choline ⟶ (betaine) (B$_{12}$) (folate)

↓

s-adenosylmethionine
(SAM-e)

↓

homocysteine ⟶ cysteine
(B$_6$)

A number of substances are required to cycle homocysteine: B-12, B-6, folate, choline, betaine (a metabolite of choline), and SAM-e. These compounds are called *methyl donors* because they release methyl groups to other molecules. Each methyl donor has unique yet interacting properties that lend efficiency to the chemical process. Limit one nutrient and the entire balanced metabolic pathway may go awry.

For example, Jean Hung and associates reported that lower folate availability influences choline status. Eunyoung Cho and colleagues found that higher intakes of dietary choline were related to lower homocysteine concentrations, independent of B-vitamin intake. SAM-e, the star methyl donor, decreases with age and may need replacement to control homocysteine.

A growing concern is the use of individual supplements of the B-vitamins. In an experiment conducted by Marta Ebbing and colleagues, interventions with folic acid supplements, 0.8 mg per day, in cardiac patients with elevated homocysteine resulted in a rise in cancer risk and no benefits to the heart. From a mound of literature evaluating many vitamins and antioxidants, smart nutrition is based on food. A balance of all donors is considered in the grocery list at the end of this chapter.

Toxic mineral alert

Be smart about the toxic minerals in food and supplements. Heavy metals are stored in the brain. The nervous system is considered the most sensitive to toxicity. Cardiovascular changes, however,  can indirectly contribute to further cognitive decline as mercury can accelerate the narrowing of blood vessels serving the brain.

Mercury is, by far, the most toxic of the metals, especially in the fetal brain. Converted to methyl mercury by microorganisms in water, this organic format of mercury accumulates in predatory fish. The longer the fish lives, the greater the amount of mercury stored in its flesh. Eat mercury-laden fish and methyl mercury easily crosses the blood-brain barrier where it may become trapped.

The fish with the highest mercury content are swordfish, shark, king mackerel, and tile fish from Mexico. None of these is recommended for women who are pregnant or lactating or for children under the age of five years. For a complete listing and guidelines: www.americanheart.org/ or www.cfsan.fda.gov/

Although methyl mercury is the predominant toxic format, inorganic mercury can slowly accumulate in the central nervous system as well. Insoluble mercury-selenium complexes produce severe brain damage. Another warning: Avoid an excess intake of selenium as a supplement. An excess intake of iron, copper, or zinc as a supplement is no better.

lipoic acid chelate

$$S \text{——} S \text{----} M \text{ - mineral}$$

> **What's the Point?**
> *The protein transferrin crosses the blood-brain barrier carrying iron to neurons. The only limit to the amount of iron transferred to the brain is your consumption as food and pills. If excess iron is continually consumed, brain toxicity is possible.*

Metal chelators, such as lipoic acid, may help to inactivate mineral deposits in the brain. In fact, the entire antioxidant network, discussed in Chapter Four, aids the neutralization of toxic substances in the brain.

Researchers I. Shcherbatykhl and D. O. Carpenter report no direct causal role of mineral deposits, including aluminum, in Alzheimer's disease. Epidemiological evidence does suggest, however, that elevated levels of mineral deposits in the brain may be linked to the progression of this disease.

Smart Nutrition, a Summary

Reflecting on the number of nutrients that may play a protective role against Alzheimer's disease, it is important to develop a plan of action. Is it best to install a medicine cabinet to store all the individual nutrients consumers are encouraged to purchase for a hungry brain? Michael Pollan, author of *In Defense of Food*, offers a simple, safe, and effective approach: "Eat food, not too much, mostly plants." Pollan emphasizes that a nutrient works cooperatively with other elements in its environment---food.

How many mid-life and aging persons consume sufficient amounts of healthful food? Self-neglect is common and is related to cognitive decline. Self neglecters are more likely than age-matched and gender-matched controls to have high levels of homocysteine, low levels of the antioxidant enzyme superoxide dismutase, and nutrient deficits of vitamins D, E, C, A, B-12, and folate. The resultant increased threat to mental status puts too many aging individuals at risk for cognitive decline---or worse.

As stated earlier in this chapter, the brain's attempt to repair neuronal damage will cease as Alzheimer's disease progresses. Treatment of mild cognitive impairment should be aggressive, as nutritional deficiencies contribute to cognitive decline. As science delves into the understanding of neuronal disease, a self-help era has begun in the battle against Alzheimer's disease. As reported by Amy Chan and associates, over-the-counter mitochondrial nutrients may be helpful for the aging brain, especially in persons carrying the ApoE4 gene and in cases of mild cognitive impairment.

Chan and group studied twelve elderly persons diagnosed with early Alzheimer's disease given a vitamin/nutriceutical formulation (SAM-e, L-carnitine, N-acetyl cysteine, folic acid, B-12, vitamin E). The mitochondrial formula delayed the progression of Alzheimer's disease in the elderly persons for the length of the study---twenty-eight months. The formula equaled results reported for the early intervention medication, donepezil.

Based on animal studies by P. J. Kamphuis and R.J. Wurtman as well as Lisa Teather and Richard Wurtman, a milk-based medical food with uridine monophosphate (UMP), choline, and omega-3s has been formulated to stabilize the brain in cognitive decline. This combination of nutrients was shown to increase the number of synapses and decrease beta-amyloid plaques in the rat hippocampus.

Huperzine-A is a mold used in Chinese medicine for persons with forgetfulness. It is available as a single herbal preparation, or combined with other mitochondrial factors.

There will be more nutritional offerings for aging persons as neuroscience unveils the workings of the human brain. Such formulas may hold promise in treating cognitive decline and in slowing early signs of dementia, along with appropriate medication.

Amid the array of mitochondrial and other nutritional aids for the brain, remember these products are simply supplements to smart food choices. The word is out: *Nutrition works against Alzheimer's disease.*

KEY NUTRIENTS AGAINST ALZHEIMER'S DISEASE

- Vitamin D for anti-inflammatory power.

- A balance of fluid fats---3s, 6s, 9s---for power against inflammation.

- Healthful carbohydrates, consumed in their natural state, for fuel and antioxidants.

- Sufficient, lean protein, with more plant sources and fish, to synthesize mitochondrial nutrients.

- Choline, all B-vitamins.

- Adequate zinc, copper, selenium, manganese, iron for antioxidant enzymes.

- A balance of potassium to sodium and calcium to magnesium for electrolyte balance.

- Vitamin C and the family of vitamin E for the antioxidant network.

Put natural sources of these nutrients where they belong---in your brain.

EXPERIMENTAL NUTRITION SUPPORT FOR COGNITIVE DECLINE

- Uridine monophosphate (UMP), choline, and omega-3s (Kamphuis and Wurtman, 2009)

- SAM-e, L-carnitine, N-acetyl cysteine, folate, vitamin B-12, and the vitamin E family (A. Chan, 2009)

- Huperzine-A (J. Li, et al. 2008)

Consult your health professional regarding interactions of any supplement with your medication or other risks related to the use of a supplement.

Smart Food Choices

Real food in its natural state is ideal; pesticide-free food is a good option; but wisdom is the key to the best choices for your brain. The following foods are smart choices at any age.

Foods that provide more than one nutrient are prioritized on the list. Several choices are offered for each nutrient to allow for differences in taste, availability, and cost. Red meat has not been included, as recommended dietary plans suggest only occasional consumption. The commonly recommended foods for persons desiring animal protein---turkey breast, eggs with omega-3s, and low-fat/nonfat yogurt---are placed in parentheses where applicable.

Only natural, whole foods are chosen, not foods fortified with nutrients, such as the B-vitamins supplemented in bleached flour.

Smart Food List

Nutrient:
Omega-3 fatty acids

Functions:
Decreased inflammation; improved memory and learning.

Suggestions (animal):
salmon, sardines, herring (omega-3 eggs)

Jennifer loves herring.

Did you know? Farm-raised salmon are more likely to be contaminated with pollutants (PCBs) than are wild salmon. But it may not be worth spending the extra money for wild, fresh salmon, if you can find it. Canned salmon is wild and less expensive than fresh. All five species of Pacific and Alaskan salmon come in cans, including the highly nutritious, red sockeye salmon.

Fatty fish have more omega-3s than lean fish. Oysters have very little fat but are good sources of omega-3s. Aim for two to three servings of fish weekly.

Suggestions (plant):
flax or chia seeds (oil), walnuts (oil), canola oil, microalgae

Did you know? Microalgae, such as blue-green algae, contain preformed DHA, identical to animal sources. Other than algae, the conversion of plant fat to fish fat is limited and varies with a person's diet.

The omega-3s in flax and chia seeds have a mild anti-inflammatory effect. Grind flax seeds for better absorption of the oil. Restrict the intake of flax seeds to two tablespoons daily. These plant foods are a source of omega-6 fatty acids as well.

Something different! Walnut oil is fragrant and flavorful. The nutty taste is great with vegetables, to give fish added flavor, and to add a distinctive twist to salad dressings. If you are a vegan, try the seaweed nori (in sushi) or spirulina (microalgae pills) to boost DHA in your brain.

Monounsaturated fatty acids (omega-9s)

Function:
A neutral fat, used in place of oils high in omega-6s.

Suggestions:
olives (oil), almonds, hazelnuts

Did you know? Buy the first pressing of the olive, the extra virgin olive oil, to capture the super antioxidants in the olive.

Something different! Avocado and macadamia oils are higher in monounsaturated fatty acids than olive oil. Avocado oil's bland flavor is versatile. Macadamia oil has a delicate taste and contains the highest percentage of monounsaturates of any food---but it's pricey. These oils contain omega-6s as well.

Carbohydrates

Function:
Energy.

Suggestions:
whole grains, fruits, starchy vegetables, legumes, honey or molasses as a sweetener

Romance loves corn.

Did you know? Are you buying wheat germ and wheat bran? The germ is high in vitamin E, and the bran is loaded with fiber. Consider a compromise. Eat whole wheat bread, pancakes, or pasta and get all that good chemistry in a single food. Persons with insulin resistance or diabetes will find their blood sugar under better control with more whole grains in the diet. Try a German muesli; it has raw oats. Add barley to soups. Make buckwheat pancakes. Eat whole rye bread.

Cornmeal (polenta) is part of the Mediterranean cuisine. This dish is versatile. Cornmeal is a hearty, hot cereal; slice it, grill it, and serve it with vegetables; cover it with tomato sauce as a side dish at dinner. Download recipes from the Internet.

The stanols and sterols in whole grains and legumes are chemically similar to cholesterol. They compete with dietary cholesterol for absorption and thus lower LDLs. Excess cholesterol contributes to the closure of blood vessels and thus poor circulation to your brain. Although nuts and seeds also have stanols, their higher fat content limits intake to small portions.

Something different! Mix ancient grains with the common varieties: kamut, of Egyptian origin; spelt, from ancient Persia; millet, grown in northern China, Tibet, and India.

Did you know? Legumes include beans, peas, lentils, and peanuts. Once considered a cheap substitute for meat, legumes are now known as nutritional superstars. They are rich sources of soluble fiber, carbohydrate, and protein and are loaded with nutrients, yet low in fat. Mung beans, usually eaten as sprouts, are highly nutritious. If the beans are dried into a flour to make cellophane noodles, the bean flour is stripped of all nutrients except starch. What a shame!

Pepper loves oats & molassses.

What about simple, sweet carbohydrates? Fruit is always a good choice. Honey is one of the oldest natural sweeteners. Molasses has a distinct flavor and a small mineral content.

Something different! Agave nectar is the sweet juice of the agave cactus, heated for thirty-six hours to convert the starch, *inulin*, into simple fructose. Excess consumption of fructose may increase blood triglycerides. And don't expect to reap significant antioxidant benefits from agave nectar. Use this "something different" sparingly.

Protein

Function:
Builds structures and enzymes in neurons.

Suggestions:
fish, soy (turkey breast, yogurt, egg white)

Did you know? Soy is a complete protein, loaded with nutrients and antioxidants. Soy reduces blood levels of lipids, glucose, and insulin more than do other legumes. Soy decreases oxidative stress, the chemical aging that increases the risk of Alzheimer's disease, according to H. M. Hsieh and coworkers. There are a variety of natural formats, such as tofu, tempeh, and soy nuts.

Something different! A fun way to eat soybeans is edamame, which means *beans on branches*, after the way the soybeans grow on bushy twigs. The pod is steamed or cooked in boiling water. Enjoy them as a snack, in soups, salads, or rice.

Bobbi loves turkey.

Antioxidants

Functions:
Controls oxidative stress; decreases inflammation; deters neuronal aging.

Suggestions:
berries, grapes, apples, guava, pomegranates, prunes, sweet potatoes, carrots, pumpkin, tomatoes, leafy greens, red peppers, broccoli, brussels sprouts, oolong tea, dark chocolate, garlic, herbs/spices, coffee beans

Did you know? Nearly all sweet peppers start out green. If left to ripen before picking, they turn red, yellow, orange, purple, or even brown, depending on the variety. Red and yellow are the nutritional powerhouses.

Speaking of greens, dried grasses and juices of grasses are sold as miracle foods. But you get more antioxidants in a few spinach leaves than in a serving of grass. The vitamin and mineral content in grass is small, and chlorophyll is plentiful in all green plants.

Apples may not always keep the doctor away, but they are a staple plant food in the diet. Apples, especially red delicious, offer a hefty portion of the polyphenol quercetin and other phytochemicals. Because the skin provides half of the antioxidants, purchase organic varieties when possible or wash them thoroughly and eat the skins. F. Tchantchou and group found that aged mice are protected from cognitive decline when fed apple juice concentrate. Still, the juice is loaded with calories. Eat apples.

A berry a day is not quite enough, but a cup of berries or cherries just may keep dementia at bay, and that includes the cocoa bean---a red berry. Berries are

loaded with antioxidants and anti-inflammatory chemicals. Studies tout the positive effect of berries on memory and recommend a serving a day. Frozen berries/cherries, no added sugar, are great year-round on French toast and pancakes.

The mini horses love apples.

**Angel loves
sunflower seeds.**

Loss of sight accelerates cognitive decline. Foods rich in the carotenoids lutein and zeaxanthin, along with vitamin E, may decrease the likelihood of developing macular degeneration. There is a significant amount of lutein in red peppers and a good source of zeaxanthin in orange peppers. And for vitamin E, remember olive oil, almonds, and sunflower seeds. They're all on the grocery list.

Bottoms up when it's a cup of tea. Oolong tea is semi-fermented, falling somewhere between green and black tea in intensity, with a smoky, floral flavor. Oolong is Andrew Weil's favorite brew, but all green and black varieties are good choices. About four to six cups of tea a week showed reduced risk of cognitive impairment, as reported by the researchers at the University of California, Berkeley.

Experts at Tufts University report that cardiovascular health benefits and anti-tumor effects require a greater load of antioxidants, five to six cups of green tea per day. Data from the Singapore Chinese Health Study with 63,000 Chinese adults found that drinking ordinary black tea, as little as one cup on three days out of four, can reduce your risk of developing Parkinson's disease by as much as seventy-one percent. How tea blocks the disease is unknown.

Something different! White tea includes the bud of the plant and the leaf, and is, like green tea, unfermented. There are lots of antioxidants in these buds. The buds are withered and air-dried, resulting in a light, clean, and slightly sweet cup of tea.

Let's not forget the coffee bean. It's a red berry, until it's roasted. With or without caffeine the coffee bean is an antioxidant winner.

The debate about grapes---fermented or fresh---may never be decided. Red wine or red grapes: both have the dynamite antioxidant resveratrol. It's simply a matter of how much wine and how many grapes. If your pancreas responds poorly to a hefty load of simple sugar, the number of grapes you eat may make a difference. If your liver is slowing down, too much alcohol may create a problem. For every brain, too much sugar or alcohol is not smart.

Thiamin (vitamin B-1)

Functions:
Energy production; synthesis of myelin sheath.

Suggestions:
salmon, legumes, brazil nuts, brown rice

Did you know? Brown rice is a whole grain, naturally high in B-vitamins and minerals, while refined, white rice is enriched. Because brown rice retains the germ, it is also a good source of vitamin E. Brown rice has a rich flavor and a chewy texture. Oryzanol, a phytochemical in the bran layer of brown rice, is cardioprotective and good for the brain. Instant brown rice is nutritionally comparable to regular brown rice, just partially cooked and dried to shorten the cooking time. Whole wheat flour and brown rice are equivalent sources of vitamin B-1.

Something different! Pasta made from ground lentils has a rich, slightly peppery flavor and is very nutritious. Try it.

Shallot loves rice.

Niacin (vitamin B-3)

Functions:
Memory processing; energy production; metabolism of fat.

Suggestions:
salmon, shitake mushrooms, brown rice (turkey)

Did you know? Choose the mushroom that's a nutritional winner for your brain---shitake. Besides niacin, you get seventy percent of your selenium requirement in one ounce of shitake mushrooms.

Pyridoxine (vitamin B-6)

Functions:
Metabolizes homocysteine; produces dopamine; required for protein and carbohydrate metabolism.

Suggestions:
salmon, sweet potato, banana (turkey)

Did you know? White potato can be substituted for sweet potato. But who would want to substitute anything for this delicious golden root? In fact, sweet potatoes aren't even related to the white potato. The sweet potato is part of the morning glory family.

Sweet Pea loves bananas.

This root is close to perfect. The golden sweet potato provides an incredible assortment of nutritional benefits. Although it is low in fat, sweet potato has a significant amount of vitamin E. The darker the color, the more carotenes as well. Even the skin is worth eating, if the sweet potato is organic.

Vitamin B-12

Functions:
Metabolizes homocysteine; synthesizes myelin sheath; enhances memory processing and nerve function.

Suggestions:
salmon, sardines (egg, turkey, yogurt)

Did you know? While other B-vitamins are available from a variety of foods, B-12 is found only in animal products. During the Stone Age, microbes in the soil synthesized B-12. If you ate a little dirt with the plant---B-12. Society is now very conscious of sanitation. Strict vegetarians look for B-12 supplementation in soy milk, other vegan products, or vitamin supplements. For non-vegetarians, a three-ounce portion of cooked salmon, sardines, or shellfish provides the entire day's requirement for B-12.

Biotin (B vitamin)

Jonathan loves peanuts.

Functions:
Homocysteine metabolism; energy production.

Suggestions:
peanuts, almonds, soybeans

Did you know? Buy peanuts in the shell. The peanut skin is loaded with resveratrol, the antioxidant in red wine.

Folacin (B-vitamin)

Functions:
Brain development; memory; homocysteine metabolism.

Suggestions:
legumes, fresh or frozen, not canned; spinach, asparagus

Blackberri loves legumes.

Did you know? Folacin is extremely sensitive to heat, oxygen, light, and storage. If you don't plan to eat the fresh food within a few days, purchase frozen varieties for a better retention of folacin. This B-vitamin can't survive the high heat of the canning process.

Don't compensate for the delicacy of this nutrient by taking excess folic acid as a supplement. Flour and cereal grains are fortified with folic acid, and a daily multivitamin is likely to include more folic acid these days for brain health. It is wise to limit intake of folic acid from supplements to 400 micrograms per day. Folacin, the natural format in food, is safe in any amount and is your best choice for the brain.

Something different! There is a purple variety of asparagus called Viola and a red variety of spinach. The large burgundy asparagus spears have a white interior and are tender, with a mild, slightly sweet, nutty flavor. Red spinach has green leaves with a red center. The leaf is tender and very tasty, almost sweet. It's bound to look great in a salad.

Wilde Heather loves red spinach.

Something different! The beet root and leaves are both good sources of folate. The dark purple color of the root is a sign of powerful antioxidants. Beets are also a good source of uridine monophosphate. Human brain cells exposed to this nutrient show increased growth and branching of axons and dendrites.

The combination of uridine monophosphate, choline, and omega-3s is now incorporated in nutritional boosters for persons with cognitive decline.

Try whole food first. Incorporate shredded, raw beets into a salad or coleslaw. Chop cooked beets and avocado, toss in vinaigrette, and you have a tasty salad. Serve with salmon for omega-3s and choline. This is the natural formula.

Choline

Functions:
Memory; learning; acetylcholine synthesis; anti-inflammatory effects.

Suggestions:
salmon, soybeans, quinoa (egg yolk)

Something different! Quinoa, pronounced KEEN-wah, is a grain-like product recently introduced in the United States. Native to the Peruvian and Bolivian highlands, the germ of quinoa forms a band on the outside of each grain. When cooked, the germ has a crescent-shaped tail that adds texture to the grain. Quinoa is loaded with brain-healthy potassium, vitamin E, iron, magnesium, and zinc. The presence of the amino acid lysine, often absent in plants, makes it one of the best sources of plant protein.

Vitamin C

Function:
Part of the brain's antioxidant network.

Suggestions:
peppers, oranges, kiwifruit, broccoli

Poco loves broccoli.

Did you know? Kiwifruit is an all-around nutritious fruit, supplying 166 percent of vitamin C needs in one serving. Equal in vitamin C is the sweet pepper, with hot peppers not far behind in rank. All peppers have newly identified anti-inflammatory chemicals as well. The National Institutes of Health recommends increasing consumption of fruits and vegetables high in vitamin C to protect against stroke and the accompanying increased risk of Alzheimer's disease after a stroke.

All fruits and vegetables have some vitamin C. Eat them as a whole food to retain all the fiber and antioxidants. Aim for five to nine servings of fruits and vegetables a day to saturate all neurons with "C".

Something different! One cup of cooked kohlrabi---the cabbage family---provides 99 percent of your daily need for vitamin C and some vitamin E as well. The cooked leaves have a kale/collard taste. The bulb is sweeter and more crisp than turnips and is an alternative to cabbage slaw. Mash them as a potato alternative.

Vitamin D

Functions:
Decreases oxidative stress and inflammation.

Suggestions:
salmon, sardines (egg yolk)

Did you know? Wild salmon has about four times more vitamin D than farmed salmon. Milk is generally fortified with vitamin D, but it may not be added to milk products, such as cheese, yogurt, ice cream. Look on the label for vitamin D-3.

Vitamin E

Function:
Major antioxidant in the brain's antioxidant network.

Suggestions:
sunflower seeds (oil), almonds, hazelnuts

<u>Did you know?</u> A fabulous source of vitamin E, sunflower seeds also have a high percentage of omega-6s. Genetic engineering has modified the sunflower seed to produce 80 percent of its oil as the monounsaturated fat, *oleic acid*. High-oleic sunflower oil is available for purchase.

Apple loves almonds.

Calcium

Function:
Enhances central nervous system activity.

Suggestions:
salmon or sardine bones, tofu, almonds, greens (milk)

<u>Did you know?</u> Beet greens, spinach, and Swiss chard contain calcium, but they also have oxalates, which prevent most of the calcium from being absorbed. Greens are still great plant foods, rich in carotenes and vitamin K. A new finding: Vitamin K has potent anti-inflammatory effects that can curb insulin resistance. It's time for everyone to cook the Southern favorite, collard/turnip greens, but without the animal fat. Serve them with black-eyed peas for a mountain of folate, as well as calcium.

Samson loves collard greens.

Copper

Function:
Cofactor of an antioxidant enzyme.

Suggestions:
shitake mushrooms, tomato, dark chocolate

Did you know? The cocoa bean is a red berry, a key to the rationale that chocolate has the same potent antioxidants found in blueberries, cranberries, and tea. Cocoa is the fat-free healthful ingredient in chocolate. White chocolate is just a fat called cocoa butter, with no cocoa or health benefits, just fat. Beyond its antioxidant load, the beloved cocoa bean has anti-inflammatory factors and minerals, especially copper.

The flavonoids in dark chocolate have been shown to lower blood pressure. Just one ounce of chocolate each day might make it easier and tastier for hypertensive patients to stay on board with intervention practices. Still, don't expect your doctor to start writing prescriptions for Godiva chocolates when plants, low in calories, can provide the same phytochemicals and nutrients as the cocoa bean.

Iron

Functions:
Memory processing; cognition; cofactor in an antioxidant enzyme.

Suggestions:
tofu, amaranth, quinoa (turkey)

Did you know? Just four ounces of firm tofu will provide most of your daily iron needs. The fat, mostly unsaturated, makes soy a good substitute for meat.

Amaranth, a tiny black seed, is sometimes called a grain. This nutty-tasting seed has a wealth of nutrients. Use it anywhere you would add seeds.

Cinnamon loves amaranth.

Don't discard the leaves. They can't compete with the vitamin, mineral, and antioxidant content of the seeds, but the leaves are worth chewing.

Something different! Contrary to the rest of the bulb family, leeks are a source of iron and have a mild, onion-like flavor.

Magnesium

Functions:
Cofactor of an antioxidant enzyme; decreases central nervous system activity.

Suggestions:
quinoa, amaranth, pumpkin seeds (milk)

Did you know? All the suggested foods---quinoa, amaranth, and pumpkin seeds---need a popularity boost in the diet. Find at least one recipe for each food and get started enjoying them.

Manganese

Functions:
Cofactor of an antioxidant enzyme; energy.

Suggestions:
hazelnuts, quinoa, all berries

Radish loves berries.

Did you know? Vary your berry consumption year-round by purchasing frozen varieties, even cranberries. In nature, most berries contain anthocyanins (water-soluble antioxidants) that are bound to glucose, making them well absorbed from the gut. In contrast, the anthocyanins found in the common American cranberry are mainly bound to other kinds of sugars that decrease the absorption of the antioxidant. Scientists are hybridizing the American cranberry with the Alaskan variety to produce a berry that has a better absorption of anthocyanins.

Potassium

Functions:
Lowers blood pressure; slows nerve impulses.

Suggestions:
sweet potato, avocado, legumes (milk)

Did you know? Cheer up with a delicious avocado. The creamy texture lights up your palate and your brain. Avocado is loaded with monounsaturates, potassium, fiber, and respectable amounts of niacin, vitamin B-6, folate, and iron.

Something different! Bring back celery. In addition to potassium, celery has anti-inflammatory chemicals.

Noah loves sweet potatoes.

Selenium

Function:
Cofactor of an antioxidant enzyme.

Suggestions:
brazil nuts, shitake mushrooms, brown rice (turkey, egg)

Did you know? One brazil nut fulfills your selenium needs for several days.

Zinc

Functions:
Cofactor of an antioxidant enzyme; balances mood.

Suggestions:
legumes, shitake mushrooms, pumpkin seeds (turkey)

Did you know? You may or may not want to cook the pumpkin pulp after Halloween, but save the seeds. Toss them with a little oil and roast. They are nutritious and delicious.

Starr loves pumpkin seeds.

Smart Foods for Mitochondria

Food supports the synthesis of mitochondrial factors, critical for energy production within neurons.

Licorice loves salmon.

Mitochondrial Nutrient: **alpha-Lipoic acid**
Functions: Pivotal substance in the antioxidant network; energy metabolism in mitochondria.
Sources: spinach, other green leafy vegetables, broccoli, salmon (turkey)

Mitochondrial nutrient: **coenzyme Q10**
Functions: Antioxidant; energy metabolism.
Sources: salmon, sardines, herring (turkey)

Mitochondrial nutrient: **SAM-e (S-adenosylmethionine)**
Functions: Pivotal in metabolism of homocysteine; energy metabolism in mitochondria; decreases symptoms of depression.
Sources: salmon, sardines, herring (yogurt)

Mitochondrial nutrient: **acetyl-L-carnitine**
Functions: Energy metabolism in mitochondria.
Sources: Synthesized from the amino acids lysine and methionine; sources of lysine: soy, quinoa, amaranth; sources of methionine: salmon, sardines, herring (yogurt)

Mitochondrial nutrient: **N-acetyl cysteine**
Functions: Key amino acid in the production of glutathione, the major water-soluble antioxidant in the antioxidant network.
Sources: whey protein in milk

SOURCES: U.S. Department of Agriculture: www.ars.usda.gov/Main/docs.htm?docid=15869 Sheldon Margen, *Wellness Foods A to Z*, Rebus, New York, 2002.

Critter Diary

Plant food is important not just for brain health; it's critical to life itself. Samson learned that lesson when he was six years old. I was living in the city, where Samson's natural cuisine---grass, weeds, flowers---was scarce. Neighbors donated organic roses and cactus blossoms when they were in season. The tiny lawn serviced some of his needs. Still, it wasn't really nature's bounty of plants, even with my attempts to supplement his diet.

In the wild, tortoises eat rocks to extract the minerals needed for survival. As they constantly forage for food, the fiber in weeds and grasses, along with the constant grazing, keeps the gastrointestinal tract churning and the rocks moving through the gut. As Samson got old enough to wander around outdoors, it was not unusual that he ate many of my pebbles in the walkway. I soon noticed, however, that he stopped eating and had a troubled look on his face. X-rays revealed an obstruction of rocks, the size of a baseball, in his lower intestine. I was told he had little chance to pass this cement-like blockage.

Knowing that exercise gets the gut moving, not just the legs, an innovative veterinarian suggested that I give Samson a large syringe of oil daily and walk him at least two hours a day to loosen the obstruction. My first thought: Where do you walk a tortoise? And my second thought: How do you walk a tortoise? I devised a harness for Samson and took him to the beach each morning. Off he went in the soft sand, just following the sun, pulling me along at the end of the leash.

After three weeks, X-rays showed some loosening of the obstruction. At six weeks, rocks began emerging from his bowel. Slowly, the bolus crumbled and passed out of his body. None of the sharp rocks perforated his bowel. He was lucky.

We both learned a hard lesson. No matter how good or bad your environment may be, plant food and exercise are essential.

Conclusion

From one continent to another, the message is clear: Have you eaten your plants and fish today? If your answer is yes, you are probably making sacrifices to pay for good food. Nutrient-dense food costs ten times more than energy-dense food. Perhaps it's time for everyone to get serious about a garden, even if it's three feet square.

Brain Homework: A Brain-Smart Grocery List

The grocery list is a starting point for your adventure in foods for your brain. Copy the Brain-Smart Grocery List and take it to the store each week. As you add a brain food to your grocery cart, put a check next to the food on the grocery list. Add one food at a time to your diet.

Brain-Smart Grocery List

wild salmon sardines herring oysters microalgae (pills) *something different:* *nori (seaweed for sushi)*	kiwifruit olives all berries cherries grapes oranges apples pomegranates prunes	soybeans tofu other legumes *something different:* *edamame* *lentil pasta*
flax seeds or chia seeds sunflower seeds pumpkin seeds walnuts almonds hazelnuts brazil nuts *something different:* *peanuts in shell (eat skin)*	bananas avocados tomatoes asparagus shitake mushrooms peppers, red and orange broccoli brussels sprouts	dark chocolate honey molasses *something different:* *agave nectar*
extra virgin olive oil canola oil *something different:* *avocado oil* *macadamia oil* *walnut oil*	carrots pumpkin greens, spinach, kale, collard sweet potatoes *something different:* *celery*	brown rice whole wheat whole oats coarse cornmeal rye barley buckwheat
green tea oolong tea black tea *something different:* *white tea*	*kohlrabi* *purple asparagus* *raw beets* *red spinach* *guava*	*something different:* *amaranth* *millet* *quinoa* *spelt* *kamut*
peanut butter almond butter hazelnut butter *something different:* *tahini (sesame butter)*	turmeric, curry ginger cloves *something different:* *leeks*	optional: nonfat yogurt omega-3 eggs turkey breast

Have a family meeting once a month. Choose a date for a family dinner. Plan the menu together and include one new recipe that incorporates foods from the Brain-Smart Grocery List.

Everyone should participate in the preparation. After your dinner event, ask each member of the family to evaluate the new recipe: Is it a loser (score: 1)? Is it a keeper (score: 5)? or is it somewhere in the middle (score: 2, 3, or 4)?

NEW RECIPE EVALUATION

Date	Initials	Recipe	Brain-Healthy Ingredients	Score (1-5)

"Super Spread"
Author's Favorite Recipe

Cook one cup of dry red lentils in two cups of water until the water is almost gone. Cool the beans. (Or/drain and rinse a can of garbanzo beans, black beans, soybeans, or white beans.)

Place the beans in a food processor and flavor with two garlic cloves, lemon juice (1/4 cup), extra virgin olive oil (5 tablespoons), ground black pepper (1/4 teaspoon), and salt to taste.

Too thick? Add more oil or water. For a crunchy texture, add crushed nuts, sesame seeds, or sunflower seeds. Mix in chopped, fresh tomatoes or olives for color and antioxidants. Spread the hummus on a whole wheat tortilla, bagel, or bread, add spinach leaves or sprouts, roll it up, and enjoy.

Last Paragraphs

Before I could spell the word "nutrition," I associated food with fun at Grandma's farm in Manitoba, Canada. The summers were short but the days were packed with adventure. We hunted for the right  wild berries to make wine, dug out the tiny potatoes and root vegetables, collected the eggs from the not-so-cooperative hens, and so much more.

Grandma's love of growing, harvesting, and cooking fresh food matched the size of her garden---huge! Yes, she made fudge and popcorn, occasionally, to satisfy my bad habit, but eating anything with Grandma was a delightful experience. Her garden was a buffet of brightly colored plants just waiting to be picked and sampled. Lunch was party time, grazing in the garden together---without worry. It was all organic!

Back home in time to start school in the fall, I created a reminder of Grandma's world, growing sprouts from the broccoli, radish, and other seeded plants of her garden. At lunchtime I'd sample my sprouts and recall plucking and eating whatever was ripe in Grandma's garden. I looked forward to the next summer together, with or without the fudge and popcorn I consumed at home.

After she passed, our family started a remembrance garden in a small patch of ground the city allocated for family planting. Amid Chicago's towering stone-and-glass buildings, each six-foot parcel yielded enough summer vegetables for a small family.

The beefsteak tomato had always been Grandma's favorite. In her honor I made a fresh tomato sandwich. Each bite surfaced memories of those special days on the farm and added good feelings to the taste of the ripe tomato.

I began carrying a paring knife to the garden and sampling more vegetables as Grandma and I had done so long ago. My brain relabeled the standard fare of fudge and buttered popcorn from "meal" to "snack," and vegetables moved to the main plate---my Grandma's wish. Years later, the joyful companionship of my first dog, Jennifer, rewired my brain again. Tempting snacks were downgraded to the category of occasional treats.

Now, in my seventh decade, I have come home to nature. I, too, have a huge garden plus a greenhouse to grow fresh produce year-round. Whether you live in a high-rise apartment, a house in the city, or a tiny cabin as I do, you can grow spicy radish sprouts or pot a tomato plant at your doorstep.

Let your enthusiasm for the emerging science of nutrition lead you to the pristine source of nutrients for your hungry brain---whole foods. Because nutrition represents the combined activities of countless food substances, the whole food is much greater than the sum of its parts. One nutrient, such as omega-3 fatty acids, may not halt or prevent Alzheimer's disease, but whole foods---that's a different story.

Come home to nature.

Key References

Aggarwal, Bharat B., et al. Molecular Targets of Nutraceuticals Derived from Dietary Spices: Potential Role in Suppression of Inflammation and Tumorigenesis. *Experimental Biology and Medicine* 2009; 234:825-849.

Alagiakrishnan, K., et al. Treating Vascular Risk Factors and Maintaining Vascular Health: Is This the Way towards Successful Cognitive Ageing and Preventing Cognitive Decline? *Postgraduate Medical Journal* 2006; 82:101-105.

Almeida-Pititto, B. de, et al. Cognitive Deficit: Another Complication of Diabetes Mellitus? *Arquivos Brasileiros de Endocrinologia & Metabologia* 2008; 52(7):1076-83.

Arendash, G. W., et al. Caffeine Reverses Cognitive Impairment and Decreases Brain Amyloid-beta Levels in Aged Alzheimer's Disease Mice. *Journal of Alzheimer's Disease* 2009; 17(3):661-680.

Bartzokis, George, et al. Brain Ferritin Iron as a Risk Factor for Age at Onset in Neurodegenerative Diseases. *Annals of the New York Academy of Sciences* 2004; 1012:224-236.

Belinson, Haim, and Daniel M. Michaelson. ApoE4-dependent Abeta-mediated Neurodegeneration Is Associated with Inflammatory Activation in the Hippocampus but Not the Septum. *Journal of Neural Transmission*, April 2009.

Beydoun, May A., et al. Plasma n-3 Fatty Acids and the Risk of Cognitive Decline in Older Adults: The Atherosclerosis Risk in Communities Study. *American Journal of Clinical Nutrition* 2007; 85(4):1103-1111.

Binkley, N., et al. Low Vitamin D Status Despite Abundant Sun Exposure. *Journal of Clinical Endocrinology & Metabolism* 2007; 92(6):2130-2135.

Bischoff-Ferrari, Heike A., et al. Prevention of Nonvertebral Fractures with Oral Vitamin D and Dose Dependency: A Meta-analysis of Randomized Controlled Trials. *Archives of Internal Medicine* 2009; 169(6):551-561.

Botero, D., et al. Acute Effects of Dietary Glycemic Index on Antioxidant Capacity in a Nutrient-controlled Feeding Study. *Obesity* 2009; 17(9):1664-1670.

Bousquet, M., et al. Beneficial Effects of Dietary Omega-3 Polyunsaturated Fatty Acid on Toxin-induced Neuronal Degeneration in an Animal Model of Parkinson's Disease. *FASEB Journal* 2008; 22:1213-1225.

Bracha, H.S., et al. Diminished Stress Resilience in Institutionalized Elderly Patients: Is Hypovitaminosis D a Factor? *American Journal of Geriatric Psychiatry* 2004; 12(5):544-545.

Brain Health: What to Keep in Mind. *Wellness Letter*, University of California, Berkeley 2009; 25(8):1.

Breitner, J.C.S., et al. Risk of Dementia and Alzheimer's Disease with Prior Exposure to NSAIDS in an Elderly Community-based Cohort. *Neurology* 2009; 72:1899-1905.

Buell, Jennifer S., et al. 25-Hydroxyvitamin D Is Associated with Cognitive Function in an Elderly Population Receiving Homecare Services. *FASEB Journal* 2008; 22:299.2.

Burns, J.M., et al. Peripheral Insulin and Brain Structure in Early Alzheimer Disease. *Neurology* 2007; 69:1094-1104.

Bush, Ashley I., and Dorothea Strozyk. Serum Copper: A Biomarker for Alzheimer Disease? *Archives of Neurology* 2004; 61:631-632.

Calon, F., et al. Docosahexaenoic Acid Protects from Dendritic Pathology in an Alzheimer's Disease Mouse Model. *Neuron* 2004; 43(5):633-645.

Chan, A., et al. Dietary Deficiency Increases Presenilin Expression, Gamma-secretase Activity, and Abeta Levels: Potentiation by ApoE Genotype and Alleviation by S-adenosyl Methionine. *Journal of Neurochemistry* 2009; 110(3):831-836.

Chan, Amy, et al. Efficacy of a Vitamin/Nutriceutical Formulation for Early-stage Alzheimer's Disease: A 1-year, Open-label Pilot Study with a 16-month Caregiver Extension. *American Journal of Alzheimer's Disease and Other Dementias* 2009; 23:571-585.

Chen, Kuen-Bor, et al. Systemic Vitamin D3 Attenuated Oxidative Injuries in the Locus Coeruleus of Rat Brain. *Annals of the New York Academy of Sciences* 2003; 993:313.

Chin, Al-Vyra, et al. Vascular Biomarkers of Cognitive Performance in a Community-based Elderly Population: The Dublin Healthy Ageing Study. *Age and Ageing* 2008; 37:559-564.

Cho, Eunyoung, et al. Dietary Choline and Betaine Assessed by Food-frequency Questionnaire in Relation to Plasma Total Homocysteine Concentration in the Framingham Offspring Study. *American Journal of Clinical Nutrition* 2006; 83(4):905-911.

Chui, H.H., and C.E. Greenwood. Antioxidant Vitamins Reduce Acute Meal-induced Memory Deficits in Adults with Type 2 Diabetes. *Nutrition Research* 2008; 28(7):423-429.

Key References (cont'd)

Clarke, John O., and Gerard E. Mullin. A Review of Complementary and Alternative Approaches to Immunomodulation. *Nutrition in Clinical Practice* 2008; 23:49-62.

Clarke, Robert, et al. Low Vitamin B-12 Status and Risk of Cognitive Decline in Older Adults. *American Journal of Clinical Nutrition* 2007; 86(5):1384-1391.

Clarkson, Thomas W. The Three Modern Faces of Mercury. *Environmental Health Perspectives* 2002; 110(supp.1):11-23.

Colliot, Olivier, et al. Discrimination between Alzheimer Disease, Mild Cognitive Impairment, and Normal Aging by Using Automated Segmentation of the Hippocampus. *Radiology* 2008; 248:194-201.

Connor, William E., and Sonja L. Connor. The Importance of Fish and Docosahexaenoic Acid in Alzheimer Disease. *American Journal of Clinical Nutrition* 2007; 85(4):929-930.

Cracking the Vitamin D Code. *Wellness Letter*, University of California, Berkeley, August 2007.

Craft, S. Insulin Resistance Syndrome and Alzheimer's Disease: Age- and Obesity-related Effects on Memory, Amyloid, and Inflammation. *Neurobiology of Aging* 2005; 26(supp.1):65-69.

Craft, S., and G.S. Watson. Insulin and Neurodegenerative Disease: Shared and Specific Mechanisms. *Lancet Neurology* 2004; 3(3):169-178.

Crowe, Francesca L., et al. Lowering Plasma Homocysteine Concentrations of Older Men and Women with Folate, Vitamin B-12, and Vitamin B-6 Does Not Affect the Proportion of (n-3) Long Chain Polyunsaturated Fatty Acids in Plasma Phosphatidylcholine. *Journal of Nutrition* 2008; 138:551-555.

Das, U.N. Folic Acid and Polyunsaturated Fatty Acids Improve Cognitive Function and Prevent Depression, Dementia, and Alzheimer's Disease---But How and Why? *Prostaglandins, Leukotrienes, and Essential Fatty Acids* 2008; 78(1):11-19.

DeCarli, Charles, et al. Qualitative Estimates of Medial Temporal Atrophy as a Predictor of Progression from Mild Cognitive Impairment to Dementia. *Archives of Neurology* 2007; 64:108-115.

DeLegge, Mark H., and Addy Smoke. Neurodegeneration and Inflammation. *Nutrition in Clinical Practice* 2008; 23:35-41.

Devore, Elizabeth E., et al. Dietary Intake of Fish and Omega-3 Fatty Acids in Relation to Long-term Dementia Risk. *American Journal of Clinical Nutrition* 2009; 90:170-176.

Duda, Monika K., et al. w-3 Polyunsaturated Fatty Acid Supplementation for the Treatment of Heart Failure: Mechanisms and Clinical Potential. *Cardiovascular Research*, June 2009; 10.1093/cvr/cvp169.

Ebbing, Marta, et al. Mortality and Cardiovascular Events in Patients Treated with Homocysteine-lowering B Vitamins after Coronary Angiography: A Randomized Controlled Trial. *Journal of the American Medical Association* 2008; 300:795-804.

Eckerstrom, C., et al. Small Baseline Volume of Left Hippocampus Is Associated with Subsequent Conversion of MCI into Dementia: The Goteborg MCI Study. *Journal of the Neurological Sciences* 2008; 272(1-2):48-59.

Evatt, Marian L., et al. Prevalence of Vitamin D Insufficiency in Patients with Parkinson Disease and Alzheimer Disease. *Archives of Neurology* 2008; 65(10):1348-1352.

Fischer, Leslie M., et al. Sex and Menopausal Status Influence Human Dietary Requirements for the Nutrient Choline. *American Journal of Clinical Nutrition* 2007; 85(5):1275-1285.

Fishel, Mark A., et al. Hyperinsulinemia Provokes Synchronous Increases in Central Inflammation and B-amyloid in Normal Adults. *Archives of Neurology* 2005; 62:1539-1544.

Fisk, J.D., and K. Rockwood. Outcomes of Incident Mild Cognitive Impairment in Relation to Case Definition. *Journal of Neurology, Neurosurgery & Psychiatry* 2005; 76:1175-1177.

Flanary, B. The Role of Microglial Cellular Senescence in the Aging and Alzheimer Diseased Brain. *Rejuvenation Research* 2005; 8(2):82-85.

Fleisher, A.S., et al. Volumetric MRI vs Clinical Predictors of Alzheimer Disease in Mild Cognitive Impairment. *Neurology* 2008; 70:191-199.

Freude, Susanna, et al. Peripheral Hyperinsulinemia Promotes Tau Phosphorylation In Vivo. *Diabetes* 2005; 54:3343-3348.

Gezen-Ak, D., et al. Association between Vitamin D Receptor Gene Polymorphism and Alzheimer's Disease. *Tohoku Journal of Experimental Medicine* 2007; 212(3):275-782.

Key References (cont'd)

Ginde, Adit A., et al. Demographic Differences and Trends of Vitamin D Insufficiency in the US Population, 1988-2004. *Archives of Internal Medicine* 2009; 169:626-632.

Green, Kim N., et al. Dietary Docosahexaenoic Acid and Docosapentaenoic Acid Ameliorate Amyloid-B and Tau Pathology via a Mechanism Involving Presenilin 1 Levels. *Journal of Neuroscience* 2007; 27(16):4385-4395.

Guedj, F., et al. Green Tea Polyphenols Rescue of Brain Defects Induced by Overexpression of DYRK1A. *PLoS ONE* 2009; 4(2):e4606.

Gupta, V.B., and K.S. Rao. Anti-amyloidogenic Activity of S-allyl-L-cysteine and Its Activity to Destabilize Alzheimer's Beta-amyloid Fibrils in Vitro. *Neuroscience Letters* 2007; 429(2-3):75-80.

Hafezi-Moghadam, Ali, et al. ApoE Deficiency Leads to a Progressive Age-dependent Blood-brain Barrier Leakage. *American Journal of Physiology - Cell Physiology* 2007; 292:C1256-C1262.

Hall, K., et al. Cholesterol, APOE Genotype, and Alzheimer Disease: An Epidemiologic Study of Nigerian Yoruba. *Neurology* 2006; 66:223-227.

Hamilton, J.A., et al. Brain Uptake and Utilization of Fatty Acids, Lipids and Lipoproteins: Application to Neurological Disorders. *Journal of Molecular Neuroscience* 2007; 33(1):2-11.

Hamshere, Marian, et al. Genome-wide Linkage Analysis of 723 Affected Relative Pairs with Late-onset Alzheimer's Disease. *Human Molecular Genetics* 2007; 16:2703-2712.

He, Chengwei, et al. Improved Spacial Learning Performance of Fat-1 Mice Is Associated with Enhanced Neurogenesis and Neuritogenesis by Docosaexaenoic Acid. *Proceedings of the National Academy of Sciences* 2009; 106:11370-11375.

Hindle, John V. Ageing, Neurodegeneration, and Parkinson's Disease. *Age and Ageing* 2010; 39(2):156-161.

Hirakawa, M., et al. Age-related Maculopathy and Sunlight Exposure Evaluated by Objective Measurement. *British Journal of Ophthalmology* 2008; 92:630-634.

Hoey, Leane, et al. Effect of a Voluntary Food Fortification Policy on Folate, Related B Vitamin Status, and Homocysteine in Healthy Adults. *American Journal of Clinical Nutrition* 2007; 86(5):1405-1413.

Holgiun, Sara, et al. Dietary Uridine Enhances the Improvement in Learning and Memory Produced by Administering DHA to Gerbils. *FASEB Journal* 2008; 22:3940.

Hsieh, H.M., et al. Soy Isoflavones Attenuate Oxidative Stress and Improve Parameters Related to Aging and Alzheimer's Disease in C57BL/63 Mice Treated with D-galactose. *Food and Chemical Toxicology* 2009; 47(3):625-632

Hung, Jean, et al. Ethnicity and Folate Influence Choline Status in Young Women Consuming Controlled Nutrient Intakes. *Journal of the American College of Nutrition* 2008; 27:253-259.

Hunt, Katherine J., et al. Inflammation in Aging Part 1: Physiology and Immunological Mechanisms. *Biological Research in Nursing* 2010; 11:245-252.

Hunt, Katherine J., et al. Inflammation in Aging Part 2: Implications for the Health of Older People and Recommendations for Nursing Practice. *Biological Research in Nursing* 2010; 11:253-260.

Ikonomovic, Milos D., et al. Superior Frontal Cortex Cholinergic Axon Density in Mild Cognitive Impairment and Early Alzheimer Disease. *Archives of Neurology* 2007; 64:1312-1317.

Ikram, M. Arfan, et al. The GAB2 Gene and the Risk of Alzheimer's Disease. *Biological Psychiatry* 2009; 65(11):995-999.

Jelic, V., et al. Clinical Trials in Mild Cognitive Impairment: Lessons for the Future. *Journal of Neurology, Neurosurgery & Psychiatry* 2006; 77:429-438.

Jicha, Gregory A., et al. Neuropathologic Outcome of Mild Cognitive Impairment following Progression to Clinical Dementia. *Archives of Neurology* 2006; 63:674-681.

Johnson, E.J., and E.J. Schaefer. Potential Role of Dietary n-3 Fatty Acids in the Prevention of Dementia and Macular Degeneration. *American Journal of Clinical Nutrition* 2006; 83(6 suppl.):1494S-1498S.

Kamath, Atul F., et al. Elevated Levels of Homocysteine Compromise Blood-brain Barrier Integrity in Mice. *Blood* 2006; 107(2):591-593.

Kamphuis, P. J., and R. J. Wurtman. Nutrition and Alzheimer's Disease: Pre-clinical Concepts. *European Journal of Neurology* 2009; 16 (Suppl.1):120-128.

Key References (cont'd)

Kempf, Kerstin, et al. Inflammation in Metabolic Syndrome and Type 2 Diabetes: Impact of Dietary Glucose. *Annals of the New York Academy of Sciences* 2006; 1084:30-48.

Kimball, Samantha M., et al. Safety of Vitamin D3 in Adults with Multiple Sclerosis. *American Journal of Clinical Nutrition* 2007; 86(3):645-651.

Kivipelto, Miia, et al. Obesity and Vascular Risk Factors at Midlife and the Risk of Dementia and Alzheimer Disease. *Archives of Neurology* 2005; 62:1556-1560.

Kroger, Edeltraut, et al. Omega-3 Fatty Acids and Risk of Dementia: The Canadian Study of Health and Aging. *American Journal of Clinical Nutrition* 2009; 90(1):184-192.

Kumar, Vijaya B., et al. Increase in Presenilin 1 (PS1) Levels in Senescence-accelerated Mice (SAMP8) May Indirectly Impair Memory by Affecting Amyloid Precursor Protein (APP) Processing. *Journal of Experimental Biology* 2009; 212:494-498.

LaFerla, L.M., et al. Intracellular Amyloid-beta in Alzheimer's Disease. *Nature Reviews Neuroscience* 2007; 8(7):499-509.

Lapp, Julia L. Vitamin D: Bone Health and Beyond. *American Journal of Lifestyle Medicine* 2009; 3:386-393.

Lee, Jong Sam, et al. Saturated, but Not n-6 Polyunsaturated, Fatty Acids Induce Insulin Resistance: Role of Intramuscular Accumulation of Lipid Metabolites. *Journal of Applied Physiology* 2006; 100:1467-1474.

Li, J., et al. Huperzine A for Alzheimer's Disease. *Cochrane Database System Review* 2008; Issue 2. Art. No.: CD005592.

Li, Zhaoyu, and Dennis E. Vance. Phosphatidylcholine and Choline Homeostasis. *Journal of Lipid Research* 2008; 49:1187-1194.

Liebman, Bonnie. From Sun to Sun. *Nutrition Action Healthletter*, November 2009, p. 3-7.

Lim, Giselle P., et al. A Diet Enriched with the Omega-3 Fatty Acid Docosahexaenoic Acid Reduces Amyloid Burden in an Aged Alzheimer Mouse Model. *Journal of Neuroscience* 2005; 25(12):3032-3040.

Lim, Giselle P., et al. The Curry Spice Curcumin Reduces Oxidative Damage and Amyloid Pathology in an Alzheimer Transgenic Mouse. *Journal of Neuroscience* 2001; 21:8370-8377.

Lin, A.M.Y., et al. Antioxidative Effect of Vitamin D3 on Zinc-induced Oxidative Stress in CNS. *Annals of the New York Academy of Sciences* 2005; 1053(1):319-329.

Lindberg, Morten, et al. Long-chain n-3 Fatty Acids and Mortality in Elderly Patients. *American Journal of Clinical Nutrition* 2008; 88:722-729.

Little, J. T., et al. An Update on Huperzine A as a Treatment for Alzheimer's Disease. *Expert Opinion about Investigational Drugs* 2008; 17(2): 209-215.

Lu, Zhong-Lin. Fast Decay of Iconic Memory in Observers with Mild Cognitive Impairments. *Proceedings of the National Academy of Sciences* 2005; 102(5):1797-1802.

Luchsinger, Jose A., et al. Relation of Higher Folate Intake to Lower Risk of Alzheimer Disease in the Elderly. *Archives of Neurology* 2007; 64:86-92.

Lukiw, Walter J., et al. A Role for Docosahexaenoic Acid-derived Neuroprotectin D1 in Neural Cell Survival and Alzheimer Disease. *Journal of Clinical Investigation* 2005; 115(10):2774-2783.

Ma, Qiu-Lan, et al. B-Amyloid Oligomers Induce Phosphorylation of Tau and Inactivation of Insulin Receptor Substrate via C-Jun N-Terminal Kinase Signaling: Suppression by Omega-3 Fatty Acids and Curcumin. *Journal of Neuroscience* 2009; 29(28):9078-9089.

Ma, Yingying, et al. Effects of Walnut Consumption on Endothelial Function in Type 2 Diabetes: A Randomized, Controlled, Cross-over Trial. *Diabetes Care* 2009; 10.2337/dc09-1156.

Maki, Kevin C., et al. Green Tea Catechin Consumption Enhances Exercise-induced Abdominal Fat Loss in Overweight and Obese Adults. *Journal of Nutrition* 2009; 139:264-270.

McCann, Joyce, and Bruce N. Ames. Is There Convincing Biological or Behavioral Evidence Linking Vitamin D Deficiency to Brain Dysfunction? *FASEB Journal* 2008; 22:982-1001.

Mellott, Tiffany J., et al. Prenatal Choline Availability Modulates Hippocampal and Cerebral Cortical Gene Expression. *FASEB Journal* 2007; 21:1311-1323.

Michel, Jean-Pierre, et al. Medical Challenges of Improving the Quality of a Longer Life. *Journal of the American Medical Association* 2008; 299:688-690.

Key References (cont'd)

Mingaud, Frederique, et al. Retinoid Hyposignaling Contributes to Aging-related Decline in Hippocampal Function in Short-term/Working Memory Organization and Long-term Declarative Memory Encoding in Mice. *Journal of Neuroscience* 2008; 28(1):279-291.

Morris, M.C., et al. Dietary Copper and High Saturated and Trans Fat Intakes Associated with Cognitive Decline. *Archives of Neurology* 2006; 63(8):1085-1088.

Morris, Martha Savaria, et al. Folate and Vitamin B-12 Status in Relation to Anemia, Macrocytosis, and Cognitive Impairment in Older Americans in the Age of Folic Acid Fortification. *American Journal of Clinical Nutrition* 2007; 85(1):193-200.

Mutter, J., et al. Mercury and Alzheimer's Disease. *Fortschritte der Neurologie - Psychiatrie* 2007; 75(9):528-538.

Navarro, Ana, et al. Hippocampal Mitochondrial Dysfunction in Rat Aging. *American Journal of Physiology - Regulatory, Integrative, and Comparative Physiology* 2008; 294:R501-R509.

Ng, Tzi-Pin, et al. Curry Consumption and Cognitive Function in the Elderly. *American Journal of Epidemiology* 2006; 164:898-906.

Niculescu, Mihai D., et al. Dietary Choline Deficiency Alters Global and Gene-specific DNA Methylation in the Developing Hippocampus of Mouse Fetal Brains. *FASEB Journal* 2006; 20:43-49.

Norris, Christopher M., et al. Calcineurin Triggers Reactive/Inflammatory Processes in Astrocytes and Is Upregulated in Aging and Alzheimer's Models. *Journal of Neuroscience* 2005; 25(18):4649-4658.

Nurk, Eha, et al. Intake of Flavonoid-rich Wine, Tea, and Chocolate by Elderly Men and Women Is Associated with Better Cognitive Test Performance. *Journal of Nutrition* 2009; 139:120-127.

O'Keefe, James H., et al. Dietary Strategies for Improving Post-prandial Glucose, Lipids, Inflammation, and Cardiovascular Health. *Journal of the American College of Cardiology* 2008; 51:249-255.

Petersen, Kitt Falk, et al. The Role of Skeletal Muscle Insulin Resistance in the Pathogenesis of the Metabolic Syndrome. *Proceedings of the National Academy of Sciences* 2007; 104(31):12587-12594.

Petersen, Ronald C., et al. Neuropathologic Features of Amnestic Mild Cognitive Impairment. *Archives of Neurology* 2006; 63:665-672.

Petursdottir, Anna L., et al. Effect of Dietary n-3 Polyunsaturated Fatty Acids on Brain Lipid Fatty Acid Composition, Learning Ability, and Memory of Senescence-accelerated Mouse. *Journals of Gerontology Series A: Biological Sciences and Medical Sciences* 2008; 63:1153-1160.

Pfeiffer, Christine M., et al. Trends in Blood Folate and Vitamin B-12 Concentrations in the United States, 1988-2004. *American Journal of Clinical Nutrition* 2007; 86(3):718-727.

Phillips, K.M., et al. Phytosterol Composition of Nuts and Seeds Commonly Consumed in the United States. *Journal of Agriculture and Food Chemistry* 2005; 53(24):9436-45.

Planel, Emmanuel, et al. Insulin Dysfunction Induces In Vivo Tau Hyperphosphorylation through Distinct Mechanisms. *Journal of Neuroscience* 2007; 27:13635-13648.

Prettyman, Richard J. Too Little, Too Late? *British Medical Journal* 2007; 334:1071.

Rabaneda, Luis G., et al. Homocysteine Inhibits Proliferation of Neuronal Precursors in the Mouse Adult Brain by Impairing the Basic Fibroblast Growth Factor Signaling Cascade and Reducing Extracellular Regulated Kinase 1/2-dependent Cyclin E Expression. *FASEB Journal* 2008; 22:3823-3835.

Raman, Gowri, et al. Heterogeneity and Lack of Good Quality Studies Limit Association between Folate, Vitamins B-6 and B-12, and Cognitive Function. *Journal of Nutrition* 2007; 137:1789-1794.

Ramasamy, Ravichandran, et al. RAGE: Therapeutic Target and Biomarker of the Inflammatory Response: The Evidence Mounts. *Journal of Leukocyte Biology* 2009; 86:505-512.

Ramirez-Lorca, R., et al. GAB2 Gene Does Not Modify the Risk of Alzheimer's Disease in Spanish ApoE4 Carriers. *Journal of Nutrition, Health, and Aging* 2009; 13(3):214-219.

Reddy, V. P., et al. Oxidative Stress in Diabetes and Alzheimer's Disease. *Journal of Alzheimer's Disease* 2009; 16(4):763-774.

Key References (cont'd)

Reiman, E.M., et al. GAB2 Alleles Modify Alzheimer's Risk in APOE epsilon4 Carriers. *Neuron* 2007; 54(5):713-720.

Remington, Ruth, et al. Efficacy of a Vitamin/Nutriceutical Formulation for Moderate-stage to Later-stage Alzheimer's Disease: A Placebo-controlled Pilot Study. *American Journal of Alzheimer's Disease and Other Dementias* 2009; 24:27-33.

Roberson, E.D., and L. Mucke. 100 Years and Counting: Prospects for Defeating Alzheimer's Disease. *Science* 2006; 314:781-784.

Satia, Jessie A., et. al. Long-term Use of Beta-carotene, Retinol, Lycopene, and Lutein Supplements and Lung Cancer Risk: From the VITamins And Lifestyle (VITAL) Study. *American Journal of Epidemiology* 2009; 169:815-828.

Scheff, S.W., et al. Synaptic Alterations in CA1 in Mild Alzheimer Disease and Mild Cognitive Impairment. *Neurology* 2007; 68:1501-1508.

Selhub, Jacob, et al. In Vitamin B12 Deficiency, Higher Serum Folate Is Associated with Increased Total Homocysteine and Methylmalonic Acid Concentrations. *Proceedings of the National Academy of Sciences* 2007; 104:19995-20000.

Seymour, E. Mitchell, et al. Cherry-enriched Diets Reduce Metabolic Syndrome and Oxidative Stress in Lean Dahl-SS Rats. *FASEB Journal* 2007; 21:A103.

Shcherbatykh, I., and D.O. Carpenter. The Role of Metals in the Etiology of Alzheimer's Disease. *Journal of Alzheimer's Disease* 2007; 11(2):191-205.

Shoelson, S. E., and A. Goldfine. Getting Away from Glucose: Fanning the Flames of Obesity-induced Inflammation. *Natural Medicine* 2009; 15(4):373-374.

Singh-Manoux, Archana, et al. Low HDL Cholesterol Is a Risk Factor for Deficit and Decline in Memory in Midlife: The Whitehall II Study. *Arteriosclerosis, Thrombosis, and Vascular Biology* 2008; 28:1556-1562.

Smith, Scott M., et al. Nutritional Status Is Altered in the Self-Neglecting Elderly. *Journal of Nutrition* 2006; 136:2534-2541.

Solfrizzi, V., et al. Dietary Fatty Acids, Age-related Cognitive Decline, and Mild Cognitive Impairment. *Journal of Nutrition, Health & Aging* 2008; 12(6):382-386.

Song, Cai, et al. Long-chain Polyunsaturated Fatty Acids Modulate Interleukin-1B-induced Changes in Behavior, Monoaminergic Neurotransmitters, and Brain Inflammation in Rats. *Journal of Nutrition* 2008; 138:954-963.

Steele, M., et al. The Molecular Basis of the Prevention of Alzheimer's Disease through Healthy Nutrition. *Experimental Gerontology* 2007; 42(1-2):28-36.

Stein, Pamela Sparks, et al. Tooth Loss, Dementia and Neuropathology in the Nun Study. *Journal of the American Dental Association* 2007; 138:1314-1322.

Stewart, Robert, et. al. Twenty-six-year Change in Total Cholesterol Levels and Incident Dementia: The Honolulu-Asia Aging Study. *Archives of Neurology* 2007; 64(1):103-107.

Tan, Louis C., et al. Differential Effects of Black versus Green Tea on Risk of Parkinson's Disease in the Singapore Chinese Health Study. *American Journal of Epidemiology* 2008; 167:553-560.

Taubert, Dirk, et al. Effects of Low Habitual Cocoa Intake on Blood Pressure and Bioactive Nitric Oxide. *Journal of the American Medical Association* 2007; 298:49-60.

Tchantchou, F., and T.B. Shea. Folate Deprivation, the Methionine Cycle, and Alzheimer's Disease. *Vitamins and Hormones* 2008; 79:83-97.

Tchantchou, F., et al. Apple Juice Concentrate Presents Oxidative Damage and Impaired Maze Performance in Aged Mice. *Journal of Alzheimer's Disease* 2005; 8(3):283-287.

Teather, Lisa A., and Richard J. Wurtman. Chronic Administration of UMP Ameliorates the Impairment of Hippocampal-dependent Memory in Impoverished Rats. *Journal of Nutrition* 2006; 136:2834-2837.

Troen, Aron M., et al. Cognitive Impairment in Folate-deficient Rats Corresponds to Depleted Brain Phosphatidylcholine and Is Prevented by Dietary Methionine without Lowering Plasma Homocysteine. *Journal of Nutrition* 2008; 138:2502-2509.

Truchot, L., et al. Up-regulation of Hippocampal Serotonin Metabolism in Mild Cognitive Impairment. *Neurology* 2007; 69:1012-1017.

U.S. National Institutes of Health, National Institute on Aging. Alzheimer's Disease Genetics Fact Sheet. NIH Publication No. 08-6424, September 19, 2009.

Key References (cont'd)

Uchino, A., et al. Manganese Accumulation in the Brain: MR Imaging. *Neuroradiology* 2007; 49(9):715-20.

van de Rest, O., et al. Effect of Fish Oil on Cognitive Performance in Older Subjects: A Randomized, Controlled Trial. *Neurology* 2008; 71:430-438.

Van der Beek, Eline M., et al. The Potential Role of Nutritional Components in the Management of Alzheimer's Disease. *European Journal of Pharmacology* 2008; 585:197-207.

van Gelder, Boukje Maria, et al. Fish Consumption, n-3 Fatty Acids, and Subsequent 5-year Cognitive Decline in Elderly Men: The Zutphen Elderly Study. *American Journal of Clinical Nutrition* 2007; 85(4):1142-1147.

Vedin, Inger, et al. Effects of Docosahexaenoic Acid-rich n-3 Fatty Acid Supplementation on Cytokine Release from Blood Mononuclear Leukocytes: The OmegAD Study. *American Journal of Clinical Nutrition* 2008; 87:1616-1622.

Villegas, Raquel, et al. Legume and Soy Food Intake and the Incidence of Type 2 Diabetes in the Shanghai Women's Health Study. *American Journal of Clinical Nutrition* 2008; 87:162-167.

Virtanen, J.K., et al. Fish Consumption and Risk of Subclinical Brain Abnormalities on MRI in Older Adults. *Neurology* 2008; 71:439-446.

Visioli, F., et al. Chocolate, Lifestyle, and Health. *Critical Review of Food Science and Nutrition* 2009; 49(4):299-312.

Walnuts: Crack Open Daily for Your Health. *Environmental Nutrition*, April 2008, p. 8.

Welland, Diane. Eat More Whole Grains; It's Easier Than You Might Think. *Environmental Nutrition*, February 2008, p. 1.

Whalley, Lawrence J., et al. Omega-3 Fatty Acid Erythrocyte Membrane Content, APOE e4, and Cognitive Variation: An Observational Follow-up Study in Late Adulthood. *American Journal of Clinical Nutrition* 2008; 87:449-454.

Who Needs Alzheimer's Testing? *Wellness Letter*: University of California, Berkeley 2008; 24(7):1.

Wilkins, C.H., et al. Vitamin D Deficiency Is Associated with Worse Cognitive Performance and Lower Bone Density in Older African Americans. *Journal of the National Medical Association* 2009; 101(4):249-254.

Williamson, J.B., et al. Baseline Differences between Vascular Cognitive Impairment No Dementia Reverters and Non-reverters. *Journal of Neurology, Neurosurgery, and Psychiatry* 2008; 79:1208-1217.

Xu, Weili, et al. Mid- and Late-life Diabetes in Relation to the Risk of Dementia: A Population-based Twin Study. *Diabetes* 2009; 58:71-77.

Yan, S. F., et al. Receptor for AGE (RAGE) and Its Ligands: Cast into Leading Roles in Diabetes and the Inflammatory Response. *Journal of Molecular Medicine* 2009; 87(3):235-247.

Yan, Shi Fang, et al. Tempering the Wrath of RAGE: An Emerging Therapeutic Strategy against Diabetic Complications, Neurodegeneration, and Inflammation. *Annals of Medicine* 2009; 41(6):408-422.

Yang, L.-K., et al. Correlations between Folate, B12, Homocysteine Levels, and Radiological Markers of Neuropathology in Elderly Post-stroke Patients. *Journal of the American College of Nutrition* 2007; 26:272-278.

Yashodhara, B.M., et al. Omega-3 Fatty Acids: A Comprehensive Review of Their Role in Health and Disease. *Postgraduate Medical Journal* 2009; 85:84-90.

Yetley, Elizabeth A., et al. Dietary Reference Intakes for Vitamin D: Justification for a Review of the 1997 Values. *American Journal of Clinical Nutrition* 2009; 89:719-727.

Yin, Ke-Jie, et al. Matrix Metalloproteinases Expressed by Astrocytes Mediate Extracellular Amyloid-B Peptide Catabolism. *Journal of Neuroscience* 2006; 26(43):10939-10948.

Yuen, E.Y., et al. Acute Stress Enhances Glutamatergic Transmission in Prefrontal Cortex and Facilitates Working Memory. *Proceedings of the National Academy of Sciences* 2009; 106(33):14075-14079.

Zhang, H. Y., et al. Non-cholinergic Effects of Huperzine A: Beyond Inhibition of Acetylcholinesterase. *Cellular and Molecular Neurobiology* 2008; 282:173-183.

Zhang, Well, et al. Coffee Consumption and Risk of Cardiovascular Diseases and All-Cause Mortality among Men with Type-2 Diabetes. *Diabetes Care* 2009; 32(6):1043.

Following Chapter Five, "Resources" lists current books
that may be referenced in this chapter.

THE BRAIN

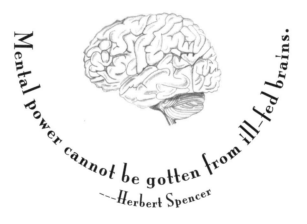

Mental power cannot be gotten from ill-fed brains.

--Herbert Spencer

Resources

Aamodt, Sandra, and Sam Wang. *Welcome to Your Brain; Why You Lose Your Car Keys but Never Forget How to Drive and Other Puzzles of Everyday Life*. New York: Bloomsbury, 2008.

The Brain from Top to Bottom. http://thebrain.mcgill.ca (accessed 7/02/08).

Campbell, T. Colin, Thomas M. Campbell II, John Robbins, and Howard Lyman. *The China Study: The Most Comprehensive Study of Nutrition Ever Conducted*. Dallas, TX: Benbella Books, 2006.

Carter, Rita. *The Human Brain Book*. New York:Dorling Kindersley, 2009.

Damasio, Antonio. *Looking for Spinoza: Joy, Sorrow, and the Feeling Brain*. New York: Harcourt, 2003.

Dietary Supplements. *The Wellness Reports*. Berkeley: University of California, 2009.

Eating for Optimal Health. *The Wellness Reports*. Berkeley: University of California, 2009.

Gazzaniga, Michael S. Human: *The Science behind What Makes Us Unique*. New York: HarperCollins, 2008.

Kessler, David. *The End of Overeating: Taking Control of the Insatiable American Appetite*. New York: Rodale Press, 2009.

LeDoux, Joseph. *The Emotional Brain: The Mysterious Underpinnings of Emotional Life*. New York: Simon and Schuster, 1996.

_____. *Synaptic Self: How Our Brains Become Who We Are*. New York: Viking Adult, 2002.

Liebman, Bonnie, and Jayne Hurley. *Healthy Foods: Your Guide to the Best Basic Foods*. Washington, DC: Center for Science in the Public Interest, 2007.

Resources (cont'd)

Lorayne, Harry. *Ageless Memory: Secrets for Keeping Your Brain Young - Foolproof Methods for People over 50*. New York: Black Dog & Leventhal, 2008.

Margen, Sheldon. *Wellness Foods A to Z*. New York: Rebus, 2002.

Mosby's Dictionary of Medicine, Nursing & Health Professions, 8th edition. St. Louis: Elsevier Inc., 2009.

Neuroscience, 4th ed. Dale Purves, George J. Augustine, David Fitzpatrick, William C. Hall, Anthony-Samuel LaMantia, James O. McNamara, and Leonard E. White, eds. Sunderland, MA: Sinauer Associates, 2008.

Panksepp, Jaak. *Affective Neuroscience: The Foundations of Human and Animal Emotions*. New York: Oxford University Press, 1998.

Pert, Candace. *Everything You Need to Know to Feel Go(o)d*. New York: Hayhouse, 2007.

Pollan, Michael. *In Defense of Food: An Eater's Manifesto*. New York: Penguin, 2008.

Rosenthal, Joshua. *Integrative Nutrition*. New York: Integrative Nutrition Publishing, 2008.

Siegel, George J., et al., eds. *Basic Neurochemistry: Molecular, Cellular and Medical Aspects*, 7th ed. New York: Lippincott, Williams & Wilkins, 2005.

Woolsey, Thomas A., et al. *The Brain Atlas: A Visual Guide to the Human Central Nervous System*. 3rd ed. New York: Wiley & Sons, 2008.

Glossary

AA (arachidonic acid): an omega-6 fatty acid that can be converted into inflammatory prostaglandins.

acetylcholine: excitatory chemical in hippocampus and memory storage areas; related to learning.

adipocytokines: cytokines (immune cell proteins) produced by the adipose tissue.

adipose: sometimes called adipocytes, fat-containing cells.

adipositis: inflammation related to obesity.

adrenal glands: endocrine glands sitting above kidneys; produce stress and sex hormones.

AGEs (advanced glycation end products): formed from excess glucose reacting with protein.

ALA (alpha-linolenic acid): a plant form of omega-3 fatty acid.

aMCI: amnestic mild cognitive impairment.

amygdala: heart of limbic system; surveillance for threat and need for an emotional response.

antioxidant: compounds that prevent oxidation (decay).

astrocyte: glial cell; nourishes and protects neurons.

ATP (adenosine triphosphate): energy molecule for all cells.

atrophy: a wasting or decrease in size because of disease or other influences.

autonomic nervous system: regulates involuntary body functions.

axon: long, slender extension from a neuron; conducts impulses away from the cell body of the neuron.

BDNF (brain-derived neurotrophic factor): a hormone that repairs neuron networks and differentiates stem cells.

beta amyloid protein: fragment of amyloid protein forming insoluble plaques in Alzheimer's disease.

brown fat: adipose tissue; utilizes stored fat to produce heat.

C-reactive protein: protein produced by the liver; an inflammatory marker.

calcineurin: an enzyme linked to astrocyte activation; regulates inflammatory signaling pathways.

caudate nucleus: part of basal ganglia complex; involved in movement.

cerebellum: called the small brain; concerned with motor coordination, posture, and balance.

cerebrum: the largest part of the brain in humans and other mammals; consists of two cerebral hemispheres.

cholecalciferol: format of vitamin D-3.

cortisol: anabolic hormone regulating the stress response.

cytokines: proteins produced by immune cells and enlarged adipose cells; pro- and anti-inflammatory.

dementia: loss of cognitive abilities with progressive degeneration of the brain.

Glossary (cont'd)

dendrite: slender branches that extend from the cell body of a neuron; contain receptors for neurochemicals.

DHA (docosapentaenoic acid): the major omega-3 fatty acid found in the membrane of neurons.

dorsolateral cortex: area of prefrontal cortex; provides decision-making capabilities.

echoic memory: memory of what is heard.

eicosanoids: fatty acids with twenty carbons; converted to various cell-generated hormones.

electrolytes: organic ions related to conduction of neuronal impulse; other metabolic functions.

endocrine: cells secreting substance into the blood or lymph circulation with specific effect on tissues.

endoplasmic reticulum: ribbon-like organelle in cell; contains enzymes for cell metabolism.

endorphins: endogenous opioids released by neurons.

enzyme: protein that catalyzes chemical reactions in cells.

EPA (eicosapentaenoic acid): an omega-3 fatty acid that can be converted into prostaglandins.

ergocalciferol: format of vitamin D-2.

fat sequestration: the storage of fat-soluble molecules, such as vitamin D, in adipose (fatty) tissues.

GABA (gamma-amino butyric acid): inhibitory neurotransmitter.

GLA (gamma-linolenic acid): an omega-6 fatty acid.

glia: support cells associated with neurons in the central nervous system.

glutamate: neurotransmitter; most excitatory neurochemical in the brain.

gray matter: a general term that describes regions of the central nervous system rich in neuronal cell bodies.

hippocampus: brain structure; processes perceptions into memory storage.

homocysteine: intermediate amino acid in the formation of cysteine; increased levels in the blood contribute to inflammatory damage to endothelial tissue in blood vessels.

hypothalamus: group of nuclei governing reproductive, homeostatic, and circadian functions.

inflammaging: increased inflammatory response common in aging.

inflammation: the protective or destructive response of body tissues to irritation or injury.

insula: brain structure responsible for bodily and personal feelings.

insulin denaturing protein: an enzyme that breaks down insulin in the brain.

insulin resistance: ineffective glucose transport into cells.

ketones: breakdown products of fats; spontaneously form acetone.

LA (linoleic acid): a plant form of omega-6 fatty acid.

limbic system: brain structures concerned with emotions; prominent components are the hippocampus and the amygdala.

long-term potentiation: series of processes involved in the formation of a long-term memory.

Glossary (cont'd)

macrophage: phagocytic cell of immune system; disintegrates and engulfs foreign matter.

metabolic syndrome: symptoms related to onset of diabetes mellitus and cardiovascular disease.

methyl donors: a carbon-hydrogen grouping that is transferred from one molecule to another for specific functions.

microglia: glial cell; involved in immune defense activities.

mitochondria: organelle in a cell; responsible for generating energy as ATP and other metabolic actions.

motor cortex: an area of the frontal lobe; executes voluntary movement.

neurodegeneration: atrophy or destruction of neurons over time due to disease or lack of stimulation.

neurofibrillary tangles: an intracellular clump of neurofibrils made of insoluble protein in the brain of a patient with Alzheimer's disease.

neurogenesis: the development of the nervous system.

neuron: specialized brain cell conducting and transmitting electrical signals in the nervous system.

neuroprotectin D1: product of vitamin D; protects the brain against destructive inflammation.

neurotransmitter: chemical in brain; quickly alters activity of a specific area of the brain.

neurotrophic factors: molecules that promote the growth and survival of neurons.

nucleus: collection of nerve cells in the brain, all anatomically identical; serves a particular function.

nucleus accumbens: a dopamine-producing nucleus of the reward circuit.

oligodendrocyte: glial cell; produces myelin sheath formed around some neuron axons.

orbitofrontal cortex: area of prefrontal cortex; provides inhibition of emotional response.

oxidation: a process of decay in which the oxygen content of a compound is increased.

Papez's circuit: system of interconnected brain structures; participates in memory processing.

parasympathetic nervous system: slows heart rate, increases intestinal peristalsis and gland activity, relaxes sphincters.

periodontal disease: inflammatory disease of the gums.

periphery: area outside the central nervous system and spinal cord.

pituitary gland: endocrine gland suspended beneath the brain; signals hormone production and produces hormones.

place cells: cells in the right hippocampus; storage area of personal maps of locations.

polymorphism: a specific gene that exists in several different forms.

prefrontal cortex: largest area of the frontal lobe, center of executive functions.

prostaglandins: cell-generated hormones related to the inflammatory response.

protectins: molecules derived from omega-3 fatty acids; protect against inflammation.

Glossary

receptor: protein in membrane of cells; shaped to react with molecules of specific format.

remodeling: the process of changing a structure or an area of the body or brain.

resolvins: molecules derived primarily from omega-3 fatty acids; resolve inflammation.

reward circuit: motivational circuitry leading to search for ultimate reward.

secretase: enzyme that severs amyloid protein into smaller peptide fragments.

sirtuins: genes expressed during severe stress to protect the organism.

striatum: nuclei of basal ganglia; striated appearance; related to movement and evaluation of reward.

substantia nigra: nucleus of dopamine-producing neurons; related to movement.

sympathetic nervous system: accelerates heart rate, constricts blood vessels, raises blood pressure.

synapse: region surrounding the contact point between two neurons or between neuron and effector organ.

tau protein: protein in the neuron associated with insoluble aggregates in Alzheimer's disease.

telomeres: nonsense DNA codes at the end of each chromosome; lost during cell division and lifestyle effectors such as stress.

thalamus: collection of brain nuclei that relay sensory information to the cerebral cortex.

TNF-alpha (tissue necrosis factor-alpha): an inflammatory protein (cytokine) produced by immune cells.

tocopherols: the group of fat-soluble molecules of vitamin E.

vascular dementia: vascular pathological conditions that cause the loss of cognitive function.

ventral tegmental area: nucleus of dopamine-producing neurons; origin of reward circuit.

ventromedial cortex: area of prefrontal cortex; blends emotions and cognition to evaluate meaning.

visceral: pertaining to the viscera, or internal organs in the abdominal cavity.

white matter: a general term that refers to large axon tracts in the brain and spinal cord; the phrase derives from the fact that axonal tracts have a whitish cast when viewed in the freshly cut material.

Index

A

adenosine, 13, 115, 143, 219

adipositis, 51, 63-66, 219

Alzheimer's disease, 10-11, 74, 76-77, 105, 129, 131, 133, 137, 143-145, 149-150, 155, 157- 159, 160-161, 163-164, 164, 166-172, 177-179, 182-185, 189, 196, 207-208, 210-212, 214, 219, 221-222

amyloid precursor protein, 143, 160, 211

ApoE, 13, 145, 167-169, 183, 208, 210, 212, 214

astaxanthin, 102, 107, 108, 110

B

BDNF, 13, 219

blood-brain barrier, 81, 86-87, 105, 107, 114, 145, 163, 165, 180-182, 210

brown fat, 51, 57, 219

C

caffeine, 41, 143, 191, 208

carnitine, 128-130, 134-135, 143-144, 184-185, 201

carotenes, 102, 136-139, 193, 197

chemical conduction, 121

coenzyme Q10, 127, 131-132, 134-135, 143, 201

curcumin, 211

D

DHA, 13, 81, 89, 91, 95-97, 98-104, 108-109, 178-179, 187, 210, 220

E

eicosanoids, 91, 92, 97, 220

electrical conduction, 117-119

electrolytes, 113, 117-118, 220

EPA, 13, 81, 89, 91-92, 95-104, 108-109, 178, 220

F

fat sequestration, 176, 220

flavonoids, 145, 198

G

GAB2 gene, 169

genes, 8, 18, 26, 52, 54, 56, 61, 68, 71, 75, 96, 124, 126, 133, 149, 150, 166-169, 222

glial cells, 92, 114-115, 123, 159, 161

glutathione, 127, 132-134, 136, 144-146, 201

gray matter, 65, 77, 220

H

homocysteine, 134, 180-181, 183, 193-194, 201, 208-210, 212-214, 220

I

inflammaging, 51, 63-64, 76, 220

instinctual eating, 15, 17

insula, 15, 26, 28-30, 32, 47-48, 220

K

krill, 102, 107

L

lipoic acid, 127-128, 130, 132, 134-135, 143-146, 182, 201

M

mercury, 88, 99, 177, 181-182, 209, 212

mesocortical tract, 21

mesolimbic tract, 21

methyl donor, 80-181, 221

Index (cont'd)

M (cont'd)

mild cognitive impairment, 76, 170, 172, 183, 209-213, 219

mitochondrial nutrients, 167, 183, 185

P

Parkinson's disease, 68, 83, 95, 128, 130-132, 144-146, 166, 174, 191, 208, 210, 213

place cells, 149, 155, 221

polyphenols, 133, 136, 140, 144, 210

prostaglandins, 76, 92-93, 95-98, 103, 124, 126, 159, 209, 219-221

protectins, 81, 96-97, 107, 108-109, 126, 221

pyramidal neuron, 157

Q

quercetin, 139, 145, 190

R

reactive oxygen species, 76-77, 123, 125, 132, 143, 163

resilience, 208

resolvins, 81, 96-97, 104, 107-110, 126, 222

resveratrol, 191, 194

reward circuit, 21, 30-31, 40-41, 44, 48, 221-222

S

SAM-e, 13, 129, 134-135, 180-181, 184-185, 201

sirtuins, 51, 68, 76-77, 222

stearidonic acid, 101

structural remodeling, 103

T

telomeres, 222

V

vitamin C, 85, 126-127, 138, 140, 145, 185, 194, 196

vitamin D, 85, 144, 146, 173-178, 185, 196, 208-211, 214, 219-221

vitamin E, 85, 126-127, 130-131, 135, 138, 140, 145, 184-185, 188, 191-193, 195-197, 222

W

white matter, 85, 109, 222

wine, 136, 191, 194, 206, 212

working memory, 151, 152, 212, 214